INHERITING POVERTY?
THE LINK BETWEEN CHILDREN'S WELLBEING AND UNEMPLOYMENT IN SOUTH AFRICA

ACKNOWLEDGMENTS

IDASA thanks the contributors to this book and the participants in the October 2005 seminar for raising these crucial questions, seeking the answers and raising the debate. We also wish to express our grateful thanks to Save the Children Sweden and the Children's Institute at the University of Cape Town for helping make the seminar and the publishing of this book possible. Thanks are also due to Hakima Haithar and Moira Levy for their part in publishing this book.

ISBN 1-920118-24-1

Published by the Institute for Democracy in South Africa (IDASA)
6 Spin St
Cape Town, South Africa
8001

Cnr Prinsloo and Visagie Streets
P.O Box 56950
Arcadia 0007
Pretoria
South Africa

www.idasa.org

Published by IDASA Publishing
Design by Liquid Amber Designs
Cover design by Magenta Media

Bound and printed by ABC Press, Cape Town

INHERITING POVERTY?

THE LINK BETWEEN CHILDREN'S WELLBEING AND UNEMPLOYMENT IN SOUTH AFRICA

EDITED BY PAUL GRAHAM
A PUBLICATION OF IDASA'S CHILDREN'S BUDGET UNIT

2006

CONTRIBUTORS' BIOGRAPHIES

René Brandt is a doctoral student at the Centre for Social Science Research and the Department of Psychology, University of Cape Town. Her doctoral research focuses on the mental health of HIV-infected women and mothers living in resource-poor communities.

Rachel Bray is a research fellow at the Centre for Social Science Research, Department of Social Anthropology, University of Cape Town. She specialises in research on childhood and youth, focusing particularly on children's experiences of and participation in social change. Her current research explores issues facing ordinary South African children living in communities previously segregated under apartheid law.

Debbie Budlender is a specialist researcher with the Community Agency for Social Enquiry, a non-governmental organisation which specialises in policy research. She has been the coordinator of the South African Women's Budget Initiative since its inception in 1995, and a consultant on gender-responsive budgeting in a range of countries in Africa, Asia, Latin America and Europe.

Mario Claasen is the advocacy coordinator of IDASA's Children's Budget Unit and is responsible for promoting a child's rights approach to budgeting through capacity-building. Before that he was a founder member of the Treatment Action Campaign (TAC) and in 2003 joined the TAC staff as the Clinics Co-ordinator.

Christèle Diwouta Tiki is an intern on the Governance and AIDS Programme (GAP) of IDASA. She was previously a legal assistant at the Parliament of Namibia undertaking research on HIV/AIDS, women's and children's rights.

Monet Durieux is an economist in the Labour and UIF Directorate at South Africa's National Treasury. She completed a BCom Honours in Econometrics (Cum Laude) and is currently studying towards a Masters in Econometrics at the University of Pretoria.

Deborah Ewing is Director of iMediate Development Communications, a South African company that provides development communications, mediation, training and facilitation services to civil society, donors, business and government institutions. She is the former Assistant Editor of the South African children's rights journal, *ChildrenFIRST*.

Paul Graham, Executive Director of IDASA, has been with the organisation since 1988. Prior to that, having qualified as a teacher, he pursued a profession in adult education. With a personal interest in formal and non-formal education, he was employed for a time both at the University of Natal and the Methodist Church

Charles Meth is a Senior Research Fellow at the School of Development Studies, University of KwaZulu-Natal, Durban and a Research Associate at the Southern African Labour and Development Research Unit (SALDRU), University of Cape Town.

Katerina Nicolaou was employed at the National Treasury from July 2002 to March 2006 as a Director: Labour and UIF. She is currently employed at the South African Social Security Agency (SASSA) as a General Manager: Business Partnership.

CONTENTS

INTRODUCTION

INHERITING POVERTY?

PAUL GRAHAM

INTRODUCTION: INHERITING POVERTY?

The message this book has to impart is simple and self-evident, but bears saying nevertheless; policy decisions which reduce poverty and unemployment will enable South Africans to meet the obligations to children contained in the Constitution's Bill of Rights as well as in international conventions like the UN Convention on the Rights of the Child and the African Charter on the Rights and Welfare of the Child, which have been ratified by South Africa. The reverse is equally persuasive – policy decisions which allow general poverty to continue and which do not restructure the economy to provide jobs will have a devastating impact on this generation of children – as children, and almost inevitably as adults as well, they will inherit poverty.

IDASA, the Children's Institute of the University of Cape Town and Save the Children Sweden held a one-day seminar on 14 October 2005 to consider the interface between the wellbeing of children and unemployment in South Africa. The intention was to provoke a conversation about the impact of a fundamental economic question – the availability and the creation of jobs – on the achievement of a national imperative – the rights and wellbeing of the children of South Africa.

In this book, one of the contributors, Deborah Ewing, quotes the words of a child living in a shelter in Cape Town who was interviewed during the preliminary research commissioned for the seminar:

> "Dear Mr President,
> I am Lettie. I am 14 years old. I wrote this letter to you, as we are children we ask you to help us to stay with our family. Help the children on the street, give them enough care and love. Can you please give our family money and give them jobs so that they can feed us enough food.
> Yours faithfully,
> Lettie."

In this letter are encapsulated the concerns of the seminar and the approach that it took. The participants, supported by this initial research and by the general approach of the organisers, took a child's eye view of the larger world of South Africa and asked some critical questions – how do the economic policy debates impact on them? To what extent are the consequences of these debates making a difference to those who are neither part of the debate nor the primary beneficiaries of these policies?

Their tentative conclusions confirm the insights of young Lettie – that while individual children need a safety net, the best option for children would be a family with an income and jobs.

This publication, comprising some papers from the 2005 seminar and later additions reflecting on its outcomes, describes the issues and notes some of the legislation and programmes that have been established to meet the needs, achieve the rights, and provide what the children of South Africa deserve. Not all the papers given at the conference are drawn together here. They can be found on the websites of the organising partners, IDASA and the Children's Institute, along with the summary report of the seminar itself.

Present at the seminar were participants from government departments, academic institutions, and non-governmental organisations of a research bent and those more directly involved in advocacy. The papers gathered here reflect that diversity – and gain from it. Insiders' views enable the reader to discover the extensive obligations under which the state labours, the plans it has made to meet these obligations and some of the constraints it faces as it attempts to implement these plans. Some of the constraints are environmental, some are imposed by decisions about policy and some are apparently more mundane – finance, administration, communication and inter-governmental complexities: the normal challenges facing any government.

At the same time, sympathetic but critical outsiders focus correctly on the mismatch between intentions and outcomes and dig deeper into whether the policies adopted are capable of achieving the goals set out or are tainted by internal contradictions or inaccurate assessments of the context in which they are meant to function.

A conversation of this nature could be fraught with tension and defensiveness, but none of that is in evidence here. I think there are a number of reasons for this inclusiveness, all of which provide lessons for other engagements of a similar nature.

First, there is the intense focus on the problem itself – millions of children continue to live in poverty despite consistent economic growth in South Africa since 1994. And that poverty is having immediate consequences as well as laying down a particular foundation for the future which may itself be inimical to sustainable peace and prosperity. Then there is the agreed rights-based framework created by the South African Constitution, which enables a principled discussion based in part on agreed outcomes, if not agreed ways of reaching those outcomes. Finally, there is a community of people who have engaged with one another over time, whether through collaborative work, history, advocacy or dialogues of this nature. In particular, the development of legislation such as the Children's Act, because of the pre-determined requirements of public participation, force social actors to engage with one another in the space provided by Parliament, which is a locus of our representative and participatory democracy.

The first chapter plunges the reader directly into the research question addressed at the seminar. What do we know, if anything, about the relationship between employment and the wellbeing of children? As Debbie Budlender concludes, the "presence of employed adults in a household is likely to improve the wellbeing of children". From her initial analysis it is clear that the level of wellbeing will differ according to whether these adults are male or female, and depending on the geographic and class position of the household, the size of the household and the type of employment – so much is obvious. She asks what the policy implications of her initial findings might be, and in the seminar it became clear that some participants thought she may be overly optimistic given the definitions of employment and unemployment she chose to adopt and the immediate availability of data. The pessimism is about whether children benefit enough from living in families where income levels are low, even if some form of employment is present. It does not really undermine the finding that there is an important relationship between employed parents and caregivers and the wellbeing of the children in their immediate care.

The same point is made by Deborah Ewing. Children understand that their life chances are enhanced by living in a household with employed adults as opposed to being waifs and strays or living in households without employment. A number of the chapters tackle the issue of child labour, invariably more likely in such income-poor households, and seek to understand how to implement the Child Labour Action Programme in a context within which economic circumstances demand survival strategies from so many – adults as well as children. Katerina Nicolaou and

Monet Durieux provide a broad framework for this debate in their chapter on developing a poverty strategy. Charles Meth summarises the challenge – which underlies both this book and the seminar:

> South Africa is committed to the modest goals of halving poverty and unemployment (poverty's main cause) by 2014. So large are the numbers of poor and unemployed that even if these goals are attained...a very large number of people in both predicaments will remain....It is clear that for children's rights to be met, a minimum condition is that their caregivers be raised out of the poverty which prevents millions of them from discharging their responsibilities.

He proposes a much greater emphasis on advocacy around the national budget and on social protection (where the majority of effort is expended) and social assistance (which receives less attention and where the impetus for a Basic Income Grant seems to have foundered, although this may now once again be on the agenda as it should be).

Mario Claasen concludes the book with a classic budget analysis which emphasises the value of the approach Meth suggests for children's advocates. It uncovers a variety of capacity issues and provokes a discussion about provincial equity, internal departmental challenges and social partnerships for delivery of services.

Embedded in this book, inevitably, is the spectre of HIV and AIDS which exacerbates poverty and unemployment. Christele Tiki, and Rachel Bray and Rene Brandt tackle this head on, the former looking at policy and Bray and Brandt offering some remarkably counter-intuitive results from an ethnographic perspective burrowing down to the day-to-day lives of a group of adults caring for children in the midst of the epidemic.

Can we make a difference to the wellbeing of children directly through the social interventions in social protection and social assistance? Or can we make a more fundamental difference through an indirect concentration on particular interventions in macro-economic policy and state administration? This debate was addressed at the seminar and should continue with the publication of this book. In its report on the seminar, IDASA's Children's Budget Unit and the Children's Institute of UCT summarised the issues:

> The point was made that what is really at issue here is trying to examine the trade-offs South Africa has made on the macro-economic front. In the context of this seminar, the real question is not about economic growth per se, but about the implications of pursuing economic growth in the way we are – and what this means for children who are poor right now.

On the one hand it was suggested that the best thing to do for poor children right now may well be to chase economic growth. This was countered, on the other hand, by highlighting the rights of children, framed in the Constitution, which cannot be traded off now for possible benefit later. It was also noted that it was misleading to pose the challenge of economic growth in terms of short-term sacrifices in exchange for longer-term gain. Current poverty, unemployment and, by implication, low demand were identified as the real obstacles to economic growth.

The report proposed that discussion should take place on "what could be done, with the resources already available for public spending in South Africa, to produce better outcomes for children right now and in the longer-term". The seminar raised questions and ideas around macro, meso and micro solutions – from whether a Basic Income Grant would work, through the thresholds to escape from poverty such as number of years of schooling, down to community-based investments in safety, recreation or public transport.

All these remained open questions, but what was clear was that an agenda had to be established which linked the wellbeing of children directly with the larger economic debates which take place in South Africa. The seminar report lists an extensive series of research questions, and these are worth reproducing here, in the raw state in which they were recorded at the time, because they point the way to a future conversation that will, indeed must, still take place.

- How do we maximise the impact of policies directed at children and improve inter-sectoral collaboration?
- Which coordinating activities amongst government spheres, sectors and departments – and between government, the private sector and civil society – are the most important?
- What is an "effective partnership"? What forms should public-private partnerships and public-civil society partnerships take?
- How best do we support the Office on the Rights of the Child (in the Presidency) to strengthen its impact on the advancement of child rights?
- Do children's socioeconomic rights in section 28 of the Constitution call for setting out norms and standards? How much progress have we made in this regard?
- What should a coordinated poverty alleviation strategy look like? How best do we get a coordinated poverty alleviation strategy onto the government's agenda?
- How do we involve children and their caregivers directly in identifying, developing, implementing and evaluating anti-poverty strategies? How may the European Union's children's commissioners be able to assist in this regard?
- Which countries have effectively solved poverty and how? Why was it possible? Does globalisation prevent this in the future?
- What is the relationship between poverty and inequality?
- What are the dynamics of poverty? What are the thresholds involved in "getting out of poverty"? Does getting out of poverty mean joining the middle class? Is there an affordable way to solve poverty?
- Are children in rural areas worse off than those in peri-urban areas? And if so, how long will this continue?
- How well are we matching ethnographic data with quantitative data?
- How do we measure youth employability in peri-urban and rural areas?
- How can we better understand the dynamics of children-in-communities so as to strengthen their resilience and capacity within the communities in which they live?
- What is the impact on children when their parents do not have access to comprehensive HIV/AIDS treatment?
- What is the impact of household indebtedness on children's wellbeing?
- What mechanisms do communities currently have to enhance their effectiveness, and how do we strengthen them? How can we deliver services to communities in a way that enhances their capacity?
- Why do we not have more philanthropy?
- What success stories are there in South Africa (especially in low per capita parts of the country) in the areas of employment-creation, improving child outcomes, crime reduction, and so forth? Which of these success stories provide sustainable models for intervention?
- Can we identify or develop implementation strategies where the resources of a community remain in that community?

- How can poverty alleviation strategies take into consideration the fluid nature of households and migration patterns?
- What are the gender implications of directing investment in job-creation specifically to Early Childhood Development (ECD) and other social services?
    - What models for the delivery of ECD are most likely to help reduce poverty and create employment?
    - What is the best way to finance ECD?
    - What is the best way to implement ECD for the 0-5 age bracket?
- Enforcing government's child labour strategy will have the immediate impact of reducing the income of the households in question. What are the implications of this for child poverty and development?
- How do we develop a mechanism to coordinate assistance and referral to deal with this impact?
- Questions about orphans:
    - How are community resources best mobilised in relation to orphans?
    - How do we best prevent children from being orphaned?
    - How do we best care for orphans?
    - What kinds of partnership between the state and communities are needed?
    - What is/should be the role of the not-for-profit sector in relation to orphaned children?

The rawness of these questions underlines their preliminary nature. It may also underline the urgency with which a number of them should be addressed. This book has been published to act as a reminder of these questions.

As importantly, it is also a reminder that the great economic debates of the day – and the policies that particular answers lead to – have implications for the most vulnerable in our society, the children who depend on adults in one form or another for their wellbeing no matter how resourceful and strong they may be. The answers that we give will determine not only how our children live now, but how our society lives tomorrow when these children become adults. Are we bequeathing them further poverty, or are we doing what is needed to ensure that they grow up free from these burdens?

Paul Graham
Executive Director, IDASA

CHAPTER 1

UNEMPLOYMENT AND CHILDREN'S WELL-BEING:
A STATISTICAL EXPLORATION

DEBBIE BUDLENDER

INTRODUCTION

Common sense tells us that whether or not members of a household are employed will have a significant influence over the wellbeing of household members. This is because most employment in South Africa is done for payment, and payment brings money into the household. Some or all of this money is then likely to be spent to the benefit of household members, including those who did not themselves earn the money. South African law prohibits virtually all employment for children under the age of 15 years, and places restrictions on employment of children aged 15-17 years. We therefore expect (and want) the majority of children to be among the non-earners who will benefit from the earnings of adult members of the household.

Income from employment is not the only source of money for households. In particular, South Africa has a well-developed social security system which delivers grants to a substantial percentage of the population. Research has shown that these grants assist in lifting households out of deep poverty. Research has also shown that even where the grant, such as the old age pension, is not paid to or for a child, some of the money is often used for the benefit of children in the household. These grants are, however, directed only at individuals with particular characteristics and thus do not reach all households that are poor. The grants are also small. In particular, grants targeted at children and their caregivers are much lower than even the amount people working in the informal economy are likely to earn.

DATA SOURCES AND DEFINITION OF CONCEPTS

The main data source used for this chapter is the General Household Survey (GHS) conducted by Statistics South Africa (Stats SA) in June 2004. Unfortunately the GHS has only been implemented since 2002, so there is little opportunity to explore patterns over time. Nevertheless this source is used as it provides more information about family relationships and general individual and household circumstances than other sources and also collects information on the labour market situation of all household members aged 15 years and above. Like the Labour Force Survey (LFS), the sample size for the GHS is approximately 30 000 households distributed across all nine provinces and including rural and urban areas. Stats SA provides weights together with the raw data which allow production of estimates which represent the population as a whole. The mid-year population estimates on which the weights are based have been criticised for inconsistencies, in particular in relation to young ages (Dorrington & Kramer, 2005). The extent of the inaccuracies should not, however, materially affect the broad patterns investigated in this chapter.

The LFS focuses on labour market issues. The GHS includes the same main questions relating to labour market participation as the LFS. However, perhaps because the enumerators are not trained to prompt for labour market activity to the same extent, the GHS yields somewhat lower levels of labour market participation than the LFS.

The two key indicators used in this chapter are the unemployment and the employment rates. Three categories are described to describe labour market engagement, namely a person can be:

- Employed, which is defined as having engaged in some "economic"
  activity over the previous seven days;

- Unemployed, which is defined as not having engaged in any economic activity over the previous seven days, but wanting to work, being available for work and having taken active steps to find work;
- Not economically active, which is defined as not having engaged in any economic activity and either not wanting work, not being available for work or not having taken active steps to find it.

The unemployment rate is obtained by dividing the number of unemployed people by the sum of all those employed and unemployed. The employment rate is obtained by dividing the number of employed people by the total number of people in the relevant age group, including those not economically active.

The definition of unemployment used above is the "official" one used by Stats SA since the late 1990s. An alternative "expanded" definition of unemployment relaxes the requirement that an unemployed person must have taken active steps to find work. This is done in recognition of the fact that many people who might want work may not look for it because they have become "discouraged" – they know that there is no work available and they are unwilling to spend time and energy on a fruitless task. Using the official rather than the expanded definition of unemployment tends to reduce the female rate of unemployment more than the male rate.

This chapter reports only on the official rate so as to simplify what is an already complicated analysis. In addition, we argue that if we are interested in poverty alleviation and children's wellbeing, we should be more interested in the employment rate than the unemployment rate as we are primarily interested in how many earned incomes the child might benefit from. Those who are not economically active, like the unemployed, do not contribute earned income, yet they are not captured in the unemployment rate. Many of the tables which follow include both the unemployment and employment rates, but the analysis focuses on the latter. The chapter thus implicitly focuses on "lack of employment" rather than the standard labour market concept of "unemployment".

Table 1[1] compares the unemployment and employment rates recorded by the GHS and LFS. The table includes two sets of estimates for the LFS. The first set is for the age group 15-65 years. This is the age group which Stats SA uses in its standard labour force statistics. The other set matches the age group used for most of this chapter, i.e. all people 18 years and above, so as to exclude children. The change in age group makes very little difference to the LFS estimates. Both LFS sets record lower unemployment rates than produced by the GHS as well as lower employment rates. This pattern holds for both male and female. More detailed analysis reveals that the discrepancy between the GHS and LFS primarily affects the African population. The overall pattern suggests less efficient "capture" of economic activity in the GHS than in the LFS.

Table 1. Unemployment and employment rates by data source and age group

	GHS 18+ years			LFS 15-65 years			LFS 18+ years		
	Male	Female	Total	Male	Female	Total	Male	Female	Total
Unemployment	25.4%	33.8%	29.1%	23.1%	30.2%	26.2%	22.6%	29.8%	25.8%
Employment	48.9%	31.0%	39.4%				50.5%	32.8%	41.2%

Table 2 explores the source of the "undercount" in the GHS by comparing economic participation recorded in the GHS and LFS for each of the detailed activities which are prompted for to determine whether a person is employed or not. The comparison suggests that undercounting occurs primarily in respect of engagement in one's own business (including in the informal sector), work as a wage employee and work on the household plot. The differences for each of these categories are relatively small and should not materially affect this analysis at the level of broad patterns. The undercount of employment does, however, add to the need to be cautious in over-interpreting small differences in various distributions in later tables.

Table 2. Percentage of population 18+ years participating in economic activities

	GHS 2004	LFS Sept 2004
Work in own business	5.8	6.6
Paid worker non-domestic	28.6	29.3
Paid domestic work	3.8	3.7
Unpaid family	0.2	0.3
Work on own farm or plot	0.8	1.2
Construction on own home	0.1	0.1
Catch food	0.0	0.0

FINDINGS

NATIONAL PATTERNS OF EMPLOYMENT AND UNEMPLOYMENT

Table 3 gives the unemployment and employment rates for men and women of the different population groups. It confirms, as expected, that unemployment rates are much higher for Africans than for the other groups, while employment rates are much lower. Further, the female unemployment rate is higher than that for males across all groups, while the employment rate is higher. The gender gap in terms of the employment rate is particularly marked among Africans, where only about a quarter (26%) of women are employed, compared to 43% of African men and nearly three-quarters (74%) of white men.

Table 3. Unemployment and employment rates by population group, 18+ years

	Unemployment rate			Employment rate		
	Male	Female	Total	Male	Female	Total
African	31%	41%	36%	43%	26%	34%
Coloured	19%	24%	21%	60%	43%	51%
Indian	12%	18%	14%	66%	38%	52%
White	3%	6%	4%	74%	54%	64%

The figure below shows clearly both the gender and race patterns. It also shows how unemployment rates change in the opposite direction to employment rates.

Unemployment & employment rates

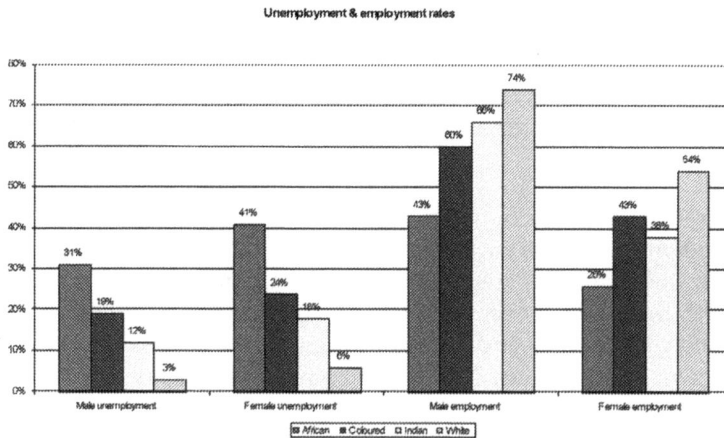

Employment includes both paid work and unpaid production of goods. In particular, it includes work as an unpaid contributor to the family business and subsistence work. This type of work contributes to the alleviation of poverty and can contribute to children's wellbeing insofar as it decreases the need to purchase the goods produced. In the South African context, there are few, if any, families that are largely self-sufficient, and unpaid employment is thus of limited benefit. Examination of the GHS data suggests that 2.1% of employed men and 2.4% of employed women do not receive any monetary remuneration. These small percentages should not affect the overall patterns significantly. Nevertheless, they suggest that some of the patterns shown below may be over-optimistic.

PATTERNS IN RESPECT OF UNPAID CARE WORK
The presence of children in a household tends to generate work. In particular, it generates unpaid care work in the form of child-care and the extra cooking, cleaning and other housework generated by children.

Table 4, drawn from the national time use survey of 2002, shows the number of minutes spent per day by male and female respondents in different employment categories. Activities are divided into three groups. System of National Accounts (SNA) production corresponds primarily to activities which classify a person as employed. Non-SNA production corresponds primarily to unpaid care work. Non-productive corresponds to all activities which one cannot pay another person to do for one, such as sleeping, eating, socialising and learning. The table confirms, as expected, that employed people do more SNA production than other groups. It confirms further that female respondents do significantly more unpaid care work than male respondents in all categories. The ratio between the time spent by female and male respondents on unpaid care work remains fairly constant across the employment categories.

Table 4. Engagement in economic and other activities by employment status

	Employed		Unemployed		Not econ active	
Activity	Male	Female	Male	Female	Male	Female
SNA production	328	260	121	46	42	28
Non-SNA production	82	210	119	349	78	203
Non-productive	1 029	969	1 200	1 045	1 320	1 208
Total	**1 439**	**1 438**	**1 440**	**1 440**	**1 439**	**1 439**

Source: Budlender et al, 2001: 39

Table 5 focuses on the time spent on child care. It compares the time spent by male and female respondents on this activity in terms of whether they have any children and, if so, whether these children are living in the same household. Women with children living with them spend over an hour per day on average on child care. Men with children living with them spend less time on child care than women with no children of their own. These patterns are likely to have an impact on the time available for men and women for economic work.

Table 5. Mean minutes per day spent on child care by relationship to children

Children under 18	Male	Female
None	2	9
Yes, but not living in household	2	14
Yes, and living in household	6	64

Source: Budlender et al, 2001: 68

EMPLOYMENT AND UNEMPLOYMENT AMONG CHILDREN AND YOUTH

As noted above, most of the analysis which follows focuses on employment or the lack of it among adults. The GHS only poses the questions relating to employment in respect of household members aged 15 years and above. The GHS of 2004 gives an estimate of 48 627 boys and 14 194 girls aged 15-17 who are employed and 34 196 boys and 32 748 girls who are unemployed i.e. wanting to and looking for work. This yields employment rates of 3% and 1% respectively and unemployment rates of 47% and 70% respectively. Ideally one would not want children to be either working or looking for work. The fact that some children are in this position almost certainly reflects lack of income and employment among adults who might otherwise support them. Altogether 81% of employed children found in the GFH are African. Half (50%) are in the Eastern Cape, although this province accounts for only 17% of all children in this age group.

Table 6 confirms that the unemployment rate is substantially higher among young adults (18-29 years) than among older adults (30 years). Conversely, the employment rates are substantially lower. These estimates give an indication of the future which today's children face in respect of their own employment prospects.

Table 6. Unemployment and employment rates among youth and older adults

	18-29 years			30+ years		
	Male	Female	Total	Male	Female	Total
Unemployment rate	41%	53%	46%	17%	23%	20%
Employment rate	34%	21%	28%	59%	36%	47%

EMPLOYMENT AND UNDEREMPLOYMENT IN POOR HOUSEHOLDS

The main reason for an interest in unemployment and its impact on children is the concern that if children do not have access to employed adults, they are more likely to live in poverty. Employment is not the only source of income, especially in a country such as South Africa which has an established grant system. Nevertheless, Table 7 confirms the strong link between employment and lack of poverty. For the purpose of this table, a household is defined as poor if it reports monthly expenditure of under R1 200. Table 7 suggests that in poor households the unemployment rate is more than double that in non-poor households. For women the employment rate in poor households is half that in non-poor households. For men, the relative position of poor compared to not poor is slightly better than for women, but there is still a very marked difference. Employment is thus confirmed as a key factor in avoiding poverty.

Table 7. Unemployment and employment rates in poor and non-poor households

	Unemployment rate			Employment rate		
	Male	Female	Total	Male	Female	Total
Poor	36%	46%	40%	38%	22%	29%
Non-poor	15%	21%	17%	63%	44%	54%

Income and expenditure are not the only measures of poverty. Another more concrete measure is hunger. The GHS asks for each household how often its child members experience hunger. The options provided are "never", "seldom", "sometimes", "often" and "always". Table 8 confirms a fairly strong, but not exact, relationship between the expenditure and food measures of poverty. The table includes only those households which contain children and for which a response to the child hunger question was provided. A total of 91% of non-poor households were said never to experience child hunger, compared to 64% of poor households.

Table 8. Experience of child hunger in poor and non-poor households

Regularity of hunger	Non-poor	Poor	Total
Never	91%	64%	74%
Seldom	3%	7%	5%
Sometimes	6%	22%	16%
Often	1%	5%	3%
Always	0%	3%	2%

For the purposes of Table 9 we classify households which report that children went hungry "sometimes", "often" or "always" as child-hunger households and the remainder (including households with no children) as households with no child hunger. The table confirms, as expected, that unemployment rates are much higher in households experiencing child hunger while employment rates in these households are much lower than in other households.

Table 9. Unemployment and employment in households by experience of child hunger

	Unemployment rate			Employment rate		
	Male	Female	Total	Male	Female	Total
No child hunger	22%	30%	26%	53%	34%	43%
Child hunger	52%	56%	54%	23%	17%	19%

EMPLOYMENT AND UNDEREMPLOYMENT IN HOUSEHOLDS CONTAINING CHILDREN

Table 10 refines Table 3 above by focusing only on households that contain at least one child. The overall result is that the unemployment rates fall slightly while employment rates remain constant for men and increase slightly for women. Among Africans there is a stronger increase in unemployment rates, especially among men, and a decrease in employment rates for both women and men, but more marked for men than for women. The increase in unemployment rates could indicate a greater likelihood that adults in households with children need and want work. The fact that the employment rate decreases more sharply for African men than women suggests that the main factor at work is not women's withdrawal from the labour market to look after their children.

Table 10. Unemployment and employment rates in households containing children

	Unemployment rate			Employment rate		
	Male	Female	Total	Male	Female	Total
Total	29%	38%	34%	43%	28%	34%
African	37%	44%	41%	35%	23%	28%

EMPLOYMENT STATUS OF MOTHERS LIVING WITH THEIR CHILDREN

The GHS asks for each individual whether their mother and father are alive and, if so, whether they are a member of the same household and what their "member number" is. Using these data we can establish which women are living with at least one of their children and investigate the employment status of these women. As discussed further below, the employment statistics in this section include people under 18 years where they are mothers living with their children.

Table 11 shows that 84% of children aged 0-5 years were reported to be living with their biological mothers, compared to 71% of older children. In both age groups a smaller proportion of African children were living with their mothers than children from other population groups. Nevertheless, the absolute number of African children in this situation far outnumbered those in other population groups. Overall, a total of 13.6 million children were living with their biological mothers.

Table 11. Children with resident mothers by age and population group

Population group	0-5 years		6-17 years	
	Number	% of total	Number	% of total
African	3 976 124	82%	6 896 415	68%
Coloured	500 665	94%	821 170	82%
Indian	121 421	99%	176 131	94%
White	424 184	98%	627 827	94%
Other	1 212	78%	5 132	71%
Total	5 023 607	84%	8 526 676	71%

Some of these mothers are obviously living with more than one of their biological children. The number of mothers living with their children is thus smaller than the number of children living with their mothers.[2]

Table 12 shows a total of 7.2 million mothers living with at least one of their biological children. Some African women are recorded as living with as many as eight biological children. In contrast, close on half (47%) of all these mothers have only one biological child living with them. These patterns are relevant for two reasons. Firstly, the presence of several children could place more of a burden on the mother in terms of unpaid care work and thus limit the opportunities for paid employment. Secondly, and in contrast, the presence of several children increases the dependency rate and thus the need for additional income.

Table 12. Resident mothers by population group and number of resident children

Number of children	African	Coloured	Indian	White	Total
1	2 734 450	328 731	87 512	273 918	3 426 490
2	1640114	242 840	65 036	261 407	2 210 596
3	770 141	123 480	20 581	75 554	989 756
4	360 823	26 750	2 898	6 541	397 255
5	130 147	6 664	895	0	137 705
6	53 318	693	0	0	54 011
7	14 141	0	0	0	14 141
8	3 215	0	0	0	3 215
Total	5 706 349	729 157	176 921	617 420	7 233 169

Table 13 shows that overall mothers with resident children have an average of 1.9 children living with them. The table provides separate estimates for the younger age group (0-5 years) and older children (6-17) on the assumption that having very young children might have more impact on the activities of the mother than having older children. (The means for the two age groups sum to more than the overall mean as the sub-group means exclude those without children in a particular age group. Only those mothers with at least one child in each of the age groups will be included in the denominator for both means.) There is no difference in the mean number of children in the younger age group across the four population groups. African women, followed by coloured, are more likely to have a greater number of older children living with them. This reflects the likelihood of larger family sizes among black households.

Table 13. Mean number of resident children by age group

Population group	Total	0-5 years	6-17 years
African	1.9	0.7	1.2
Coloured	1.8	0.7	1.1
Indian	1.7	0.7	1.0
White	1.7	0.7	1.0
Total	1.9	0.7	1.2

Table 14 shows the patterns in terms of the unemployment rate of resident mothers as the number of children of different ages increases. If one focuses on the total number of children, the unemployment rate is relatively high among those with one child, decreases as the number increases, and then perhaps rises again when the number of children exceeds four. However, the rates for women with large numbers of children should be treated with scepticism as the sample size is small.[3] Among those with young children, the unemployment rate is uniformly very high, suggesting that many of these mothers want to work but can't find work. Among those with older children, the rate tends to be lower and hovers between 29% and 32%. There are thus no clear patterns in respect of the unemployment rate and the number of children. This could be the result of several different opposing trends, such as the greater need for unpaid care work when there are children at the same time as the greater need to earn money. The pattern also partly reflects the overall higher unemployment rate among younger people (see above) in that mothers of younger children tend to be younger than mothers of older children.

Table 14. Unemployment rate of resident mothers by age group of child/ren

Number of children	Total	0-5 years	6-17 years
0		27%	49%
1	37%	42%	29%
2	32%	43%	28%
3	32%	43%	32%
4	34%	0%	29%
5	36%		27%
6	40%		68%
7	44%		-
	-		
Total	35%	35%	35%

Table 15 records the employment rate for the different groupings of resident mothers. The pattern for all resident mothers is the mirror opposite of that in respect of the unemployment rate, but more pronounced. The employment rate increases sharply as the number of children increases from one to two, but then declines again with every extra child. For those with young children, the pattern is a consistent decrease. For those with older children there is a minimal increase from one to two children, and then a consistent decrease in the employment rate. These patterns suggest that the unpaid care work burden of extra children might be affecting mothers' engagement with the labour market. The patterns are also partly a reflection of the fact that African women tend to have more children, and employment rates among African women tend to be lower than for other women.

Table 15. Employment rate of resident mothers by age group of child/ren

Number of children	Total	0-5 years	6-17 years
0		44%	24%
1	33%	30%	42%
2	40%	27%	43%
3	38%	21%	35%
4	29%	22%	28%
5	25%		26%
6	22%		14%
7	11%		-
8	12%		
Total	36%	36%	36%

The figure summarises the overall patterns reflected in the above two tables about the relationship between the number of children and the unemployment and employment rates among adults. It confirms that the pattern in respect of households with one child differs from that for households with two or more children.

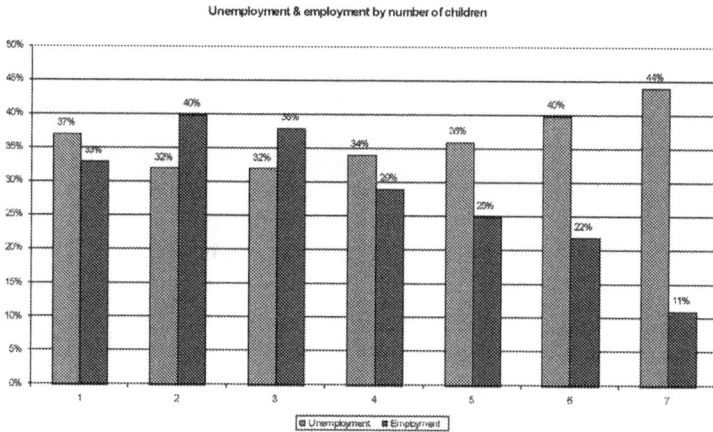

Unemployment & employment by number of children

The above patterns could be complicated by the fact that older women are likely to have more children than younger ones, and age as well as other factors affects labour market engagement. Table 16 reveals that 91% of the resident mothers are under age 50, with close on two-thirds in the age range 20-30 years.

Table 16. Age of resident mothers

Age group	Number	Percent
15-19	238 180	3%
20-29	2 246 011	31%
30-39	2 469 684	34%
40-49	1 623 976	22%
50+	654 936	9%
Unspecified	383	0%
Total	7 233 169	100%

Table 17 compares the unemployment and employment rates of resident mothers with those of other women in the same age group. The unemployment rate is generally higher among the resident mothers than among other women except for the very young age group. The pattern is most pronounced in the 20-29 year age group. The employment rate is generally lower among the resident mothers than among other women, except for the very young age group and the women over 50 years of age. It is difficult to know which different forces produce these patterns. It could be that the younger mothers need work because of the extra mouths to feed, but are less able to find work because of the constraints imposed by mothering.

Table 17. Unemployment and employment among women by residence with children

	Resident mothers		Other women	
Age group	Unemployment rate	Employment rate	Unemployment rate	Employment rate
15-19	68%	5%	72%	2%
20-29	55%	22%	49%	28%
30-39	31%	44%	30%	51%
40-49	21%	48%	17%	52%
50+	15%	32%	8%	18%

One of the other possible reasons for resident mothers not being employed involves the "supply" issue of these women maybe not wanting to do "economic" work, perhaps because of the extent of the unpaid care work they are responsible for. Table 18 tabulates the reasons provided in the GHS as to why resident mothers recorded as not economically active were not working. For close on two-fifths (38%) the reason is that they could not find work, or could not find suitable work. In effect, these women are unemployed rather than not economically active. The ones who give the reason as being that they are seasonal workers or that they were retrenched could be added to this category. Just over a quarter (27%) gives the reason that they are full-time homemakers. These are the ones who might feel that their unpaid care work does not allow them to work.

**Table 18. Reasons that not economically active
resident mothers are not working**

Reason	Number	Percent
Scholar/student	223 405	7%
Homemaker	889 970	27%
Retired	14 408	0%
Illness, disability, etc	323 708	10%
Too young/too old	164 237	5%
Seasonal worker	19 331	1%
Lack of skills	127 720	4%
Can't find work	1 173 941	36%
Can't find suitable work	50 248	2%
Contract worker	797	0%
Retrenched	13 984	0%
Other	290 046	9%
Unspecified	11 943	0%
Total	3 303 737	100%

EMPLOYMENT STATUS OF FATHERS LIVING WITH THEIR CHILDREN

Table 19 corresponds to Table 11 above, except that this time it shows the number of younger and older children who have their biological fathers living with them. Comparison of the two tables confirms that children are far less likely to be living with their biological fathers than to be living with their biological mothers. Overall, 6.9 million children are recorded as living with their biological fathers compared to 13.6 million living with their biological mothers.

Table 19. Children with resident fathers by age and population group

	0-5 years		6-17 years	
	Number	% of total	Number	% of total
African	1 583 570	33%	3 273 950	32%
Coloured	293 076	55%	544 009	54%
Indian	109 432	89%	162 578	87%
White	404 020	93%	542 354	82%
Other	348	22%	3 458	48%
Total	2 390 447	40%	4 526 350	37%

As with mothers, the likelihood of the father being present decreases with the age of the child, but in a far less noticeable way than for mothers. As with mothers, African children, followed by coloured children, are far less likely than those from other population groups to be living with their biological fathers. The difference between the population groups is more marked for fathers than mothers and almost certainly reflects the greater likelihood that African and coloured children are born outside marriage, as well as the legacy of migrant labour. For the purposes of this study, it means that these children are less likely to benefit from the employment of their fathers if the fathers are fortunate enough to be employed.

Unfortunately the GHS does not allow us to identify non-resident fathers, their employment status and whether they pay maintenance to the mother or other caregiver for the child. It is, however, well-known that only a small proportion of non-resident fathers pay maintenance and, when they do, the amounts paid are usually very small. We might expect approximately half of all fathers to pay maintenance on the basis that approximately half of all adult men are employed. This would be a very optimistic assumption as the failings of the maintenance system even in respect of employed fathers are well-known. Non-resident fathers who do pay maintenance tend to pay only a tiny proportion of their income. Thus a 2004 survey among 180 women collecting maintenance, 20 in each of the nine provinces, found that the median amount of maintenance awarded per child was R200 per month and the mean R226 (Commission on Gender Equality, 2004: 51). The employment status of non-resident fathers should thus be regarded as providing potential, but unlikely, benefit to the child unless the private maintenance system is vastly improved.

Returning to the resident fathers, we now examine the number of children that these fathers are living with and their employment status.[4] Table 20 reveals that 42% of the resident fathers are living with only one child and a further 49% with only two or three children. This further limits the reach of fathers' employment.

Table 20. Resident fathers by population group and number of resident children

Number	African	Coloured	Indian	White	Total
1	970 796	173 465	78 008	231 580	1 454 165
2	712 846	158 198	60 018	236 956	1 169 216
3	365 784	84 755	18 795	72 473	541 806
4	179 899	16 758	3 616	5 856	206 129
5	73 269	3 562	176	0	77 007
6	28 650	543	0	0	29 193
7	12 026	0	0	0	12 026
8	2 145	0	0	0	2 145
9	327	0	0	0	327
Total	2 345 741	437 280	160 613	546 865	3 492 014

Table 21 gives an overall average number of children per resident father ranging from 1.7 for Indian and white fathers to 2.1 for African fathers. As with mothers, the average number of young children is 0.7 across all population groups, while there are differences across population groups in respect of older children.

Table 21. Mean number of resident children by age group and population group

Population group	Total	0-5 years	6-17 years
African	2.1	0.7	1.4
Coloured	1.9	0.7	1.2
Indian	1.7	0.7	1.0
White	1.7	0.7	1.0
Total	2.0	0.7	1.3

The overall unemployment rate for the resident fathers is 13% while the overall employment rate is 72%. Table 22 does not show any clear pattern in respect of the unemployment rate as the total number of resident children increases. There does seem to be some increase in the rate with increasing numbers of children, but this pattern is most marked when the number of children is more than three, which applies to a relatively small number of cases. There is very little change in unemployment rates with changes in the number of young children, including no difference between fathers with no young children and those who have some. This pattern is very different to that for resident mothers. There is also little variation in the rate with changes in the number of older children for the first few such children. These patterns confirm the hypothesis that the presence of children is likely to have a far greater effect on mothers' availability for and engagement in economic work than on fathers'.

Table 22. Unemployment rate of resident fathers by number of children

Number of children	Total	0-5 years	6-12 years
0		13%	13%
1	15%	13%	13%
2	11%	12%	12%
3	11%	11%	15%
4	18%	-	18%
5	23%		19%
6	23%		25%
7	6%		
8	25%		
9	-		

Table 23 shows the pattern in respect of employment rates. Here, as with mothers, the pattern as one moves from one to two children is different to the pattern as the number increases beyond that. The pattern of an initial increase followed by a consistent decrease is the same as for women, although the rates are much higher for fathers than for mothers. There is no clear pattern in respect of the numbers of younger children except that those with some young children are more likely than those with none to be employed. The opposite pattern holds in respect of fathers with older children where the rate decreases as the number of children increases.

Table 23. Employment rate of resident fathers by number of children

Number of children	Total	0-5 years	6-12 years
0		67%	78%
1	70%	75%	71%
2	76%	78%	73%
3	75%	71%	65%
4	64%	-	58%
5	57%		58%
6	54%		54%
7	58%		-
8	67%		-
9	-		

As with mothers, we investigate the age patterns among resident fathers as this could affect their employment status. Comparison of Table 24 with Table 16 reveals that fathers tend to be older than mothers. Thus 21% of resident fathers are 50 years or older, compared to only 9% of resident mothers. A total of 6% of the fathers are 60 years or older and some of these might be expected to have left the labour market.

Table 24. Age distribution of resident fathers

Age group	Number	Distribution
15-19	4 773	0%
20-29	386 769	11%
30-39	1 248 028	36%
40-49	1 113 094	32%
50+	739 168	21%
Unspecified	182	0%
Total	3 492 014	100%

Table 25 reveals that, in contrast to resident mothers and other women, the unemployment rate among resident fathers is lower than among other men of the same age group. This could partly reflect the fact that African men – who are more likely to be unemployed – are less likely to be living with their children. The employment rate is noticeably higher for resident fathers than for other men across all age groups. This is again a very different pattern to the one found among women.

Table 25. Unemployment and employment among men by resident with children

	Resident fathers		Other men	
Age group	Unemployment rate	Employment rate	Unemployment rate	Employment rate
15-19	42%	31%	52%	5%
20-29	19%	72%	43%	37%
30-39	11%	81%	27%	59%
40-49	14%	75%	19%	63%
50+	12%	52%	11%	36%
Total	13%	72%	32%	36%

Table 26 confirms, as expected, that only a tiny proportion (1%) of resident fathers who are not economically active are said not to be working because they are homemakers. Just over a quarter (27%) could be regarded as unemployed as inability to find (suitable) work is provided as their reason for not working. There are nearly a quarter (24%) for whom the reason is that they are too old (or, unlikely, young), confirming the age patterns described above. Finally, close on a third (30%) are said not to be working on account of illness or disability. This difference from the female pattern could be partly explained by some men being at home, rather than elsewhere, because they are ill or disabled and need care. It could also be related to the age differences between resident mothers and fathers.

**Table 26. Reason that not economically active
resident fathers are not working**

Reason	Number	Percent
Scholar/student	1 208	0%
Homemaker	5 033	1%
Retired	26 285	4%
Illness, disability, etc	179 220	30%
Too young/too old	140 306	24%
Seasonal worker	4 417	1%
Lack of skills	15 820	3%
Can't find work	157 904	26%
Can't find suitable work	7 372	1%
Contract worker	2 010	0%
Retrenched	33 715	6%
Other	17 983	3%
Unspecified	5 379	1%
Total	596 651	100%

FROM THE CHILD'S PERSPECTIVE

The previous sections looked at the situation of resident mothers and fathers. This section takes the perspective of the children, and investigates whether they are living with employed parents or more generally with adults who are employed.

Table 27 reveals that 42% of the total of 18 million children in the country had an employed parent living with them in June 2004, and 59% had an employed adult (whether a parent or someone else) living with them. The table and figure show that the likelihood that a child was living with an employed adult varied enormously across the provinces. Western Cape children were the most likely to live with employed parents (70%) or any employed adult (86%). Children in Limpopo were least likely to do so in that only 29% lived with an employed parent and only 42% lived with at least one employed adult.

Table 27. Presence of employed parents and adults by province

Province	Total children	Employed parent	% of total	Employed adult	% of total
Western Cape	1 558 708	1 096 841	70%	1 340 206	86%
Eastern Cape	3 215 847	1 022 542	32%	1 596 851	50%
Northern Cape	337 192	160 903	48%	228 234	68%
Free State	1 063 842	509 765	48%	715 180	67%
KwaZulu-Natal	3 792 375	1 355 458	36%	2 019 766	53%
North West	1 488 645	523 625	35%	798 919	54%
Gauteng	2 641 736	1 666 038	63%	2 067 075	78%
Mpumalanga	1 307 864	562 842	43%	863 898	66%
Limpopo	2 615 606	749 652	29%	1 090 242	42%
Total	18 021 815	7 647 665	42%	10 720 371	59%

% of children living with employed parent and adults

Limpopo — 29%, 42%
Eastern Cape — 32%, 50%
North West — 39%, 54%
KwaZulu-Natal — 36%, 53%
Mpumalanga — 43%, 66%
Northern Cape — 47%, 66%
Free State — 48%, 67%
Gauteng — 63%, 78%
Western Cape — 70%, 86%

Employed parent   Employed adult

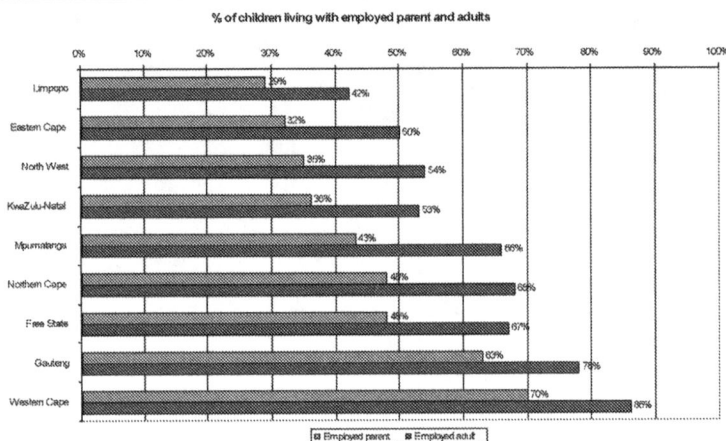

Table 28 suggests that there is only a small difference in the likelihood that older and younger children will have access to an employed parent or adult. The likelihood of both employed parents and employed adults being present is slightly greater for younger than older children. The difference is greater in respect of access to employed adults in general than in terms of access to an employed parent.

Table 28. Presence of employed parents and adults by age of child

	Employed parent	Employed adult
Total	42%	59%
0-5 years	43%	62%
6-17 years	42%	58%

Table 29 shows that the overwhelming majority of white and Indian children are living with an employed adult and most are also living with an employed parent. In contrast, only just over a third (35%) of African children are living with an employed parent and only just over half (54%) are living with an employed adult.

Table 29. Presence of employed parents and adults by population group

Population group	Employed parent	Employed adult
African	35%	54%
Coloured	65%	83%
Indian	87%	92%
White	94%	97%
Total	42%	59%

IMPACT OF THE NUMBER OF EMPLOYED ADULTS

This section take the analysis further by investigating whether and to what extent the number of employed adults in a household influences a range of possible indicators of wellbeing. The GHS records as many as seven employed adults in some households, but most households have far fewer. The analysis therefore distinguishes between households with no, one, two and three or more employed adults.

Table 30 compares the situation of households with and without children in relation to their access to employed adults. It suggests that households with children are more likely than others not to have any employed adults, but also more likely than households without children to have more than one adult. This suggests that, once again, there are several factors at play in determining the patterns. The rest of the analysis focuses only on households containing children.

Table 30. Households by number of employed adults and presence of children

Employed adults	No children	Children	Total
0	30%	37%	34%
1	53%	39%	45%
2	14%	20%	18%
3+	3%	4%	4%
Total	100%	100%	100%

Table 31 investigates whether the number of employed adults affects the likelihood of school attendance. It provides very little evidence of any such effect. Children who are beyond the age at which schooling is compulsory and who live in households with many employed adults seem, in fact, slightly less likely to attend school than those with fewer employed adults in their household. This counter-intuitive pattern may reflect the fact that households with many employed adults are likely to be larger overall, and large households predominate among the poor.

Table 31. Percentage of children attending school by number of employed adults

Employed adults	6-17 years	6-14 years	15-17 years
0	95%	96%	91%
1	96%	97%	91%
2	96%	97%	92%
3+	95%	98%	86%
Total	95%	97%	91%

Table 32 suggests that there could be further differences based on whether the employed adults are male or female. The table compares school attendance levels of children aged 6-17 years in households in which there are two employed men, those in which there are two employed women, and those in which there is one employed man and one employed women. The analysis is restricted to households with two employed adults so as to limit the influence of confounding factors. It seems that children in households with a male-female employed pair and those with two employed women are likely to fare better than those with two employed men. This pattern exists despite the fact that women are likely to earn less than men, and thus a household with two male employed can be expected to be wealthier than one with two females employed. The differences between the percentages are not very large.

Table 32. Percentage of children attending school by sex of employed adults in households with two employed adults

	% School
2 men employed	92%
1 man, 1 women employed	97%
2 women employed	96%
Total	96%

Unfortunately, the number of households and children decreases each time we pursue the analysis further in this way. This restricts the fruitfulness of taking the analysis further with this dataset. Thus 1.46 million households have exactly two employed adults, of which 82% have a male-female pair, and only 9% each have two women and two men employed. These households contain a total of 3.2 million children, of whom 88% are in the male-female pair households, 10% in the households with two employed men and 12% in the households with two employed women.

This type of analysis is not taken further in this chapter as many of the tables which follow use a subset of children which decreases the numbers involved even further. Table 32 suggests that this would be a fruitful area for further research. However, the table should not make us jump too quickly to conclusions about the greater altruism of women, or their greater concern for children's wellbeing. For example, Table 33 shows a much higher level of reported hunger in households with two women employed than in those with two men employed or with a male-female pair employed. This pattern could, though, partly be a result of greater awareness of women of child hunger if the household informant in the households with two women employed tended to be female.

Table 33. Presence of hunger among children in households with two employed adults

	% with child hunger
2 men employed	15%
1 man, 1 women employed	7%
2 women employed	21%
Total	9%

Returning to school attendance, Table 34 suggests that lack of money for fees is more likely to be given as a reason for not attending school as the number of employed adults in the household decreases.

Table 34. Lack of money for fees as reason for not attending school by number of employed adults

Employed adults	%
0	30%
1	23%
2	21%
3	24%
Total	26%

Table 35 suggests that, for those children who attend school, there is more likely to be reporting of the problem of fees being too high as the number of employed adults in the household decreases. Again the differences are relatively small.

**Table 35. Too high fees among children attending
school by number of employed adults**

Employed adults	% reporting fees too high
0	16%
1	13%
2	12%
3	12%
Total	14%

Table 36 suggests that among those repeating a grade, the lack of money for fees is more likely to be offered as a reason as the number of employed adults in the household decreases.

**Table 36. No money for fees as reason for repeating
grade by number of employed adults**

Employed adults	% giving fees as reason
0	8%
1	7%
2	4%
3	5%
Total	7%

Table 37 suggests fairly good targeting of the school feeding scheme as the likelihood of a schoolgoing child benefiting from the programme tends to increase with a decrease in the number of employed adults. The reverse of the pattern for those in household with three or more employed adults might again reflect the predominance of large households among the poor noted above.

Table 37. Access to school feeding scheme by number of employed adults

Employed adults	% benefiting from school feeding
0	54%
1	43%
2	31%
3	42%
Total	46%

Table 38 shows attendance at preschool (defined to include day care, crèche and pre-primary) for children aged less than 6 years by the number of employed adults in the household. (The data suggest that significant numbers of children aged six and seven years are attending preschool. They are excluded from the analysis as the reason for not attending could be attendance at school rather than lack of income to pay for preschool.) The table suggests, as expected, that preschool attendance increases as the number of employed adults increases. This can be explained both by increased income and thus ability to pay fees, and by the need to have other people care for the child if adults are doing economic work.

Table 38. Preschool attendance of children aged under 6 by number of employed adults

Employed adults	% preschool
0	11%
1	17%
2	26%
3	18%
Total	17%

Table 39 suggests that children living in households with no employed adults are less likely to be reported to have suffered from illness or injury over the past 12 months than those living in households with employed adults. This finding must be treated with caution as it is often found that those who are more disadvantaged are less likely to report illness of the same severity than those who are advantaged. Again, there is some reversal of the trend where there are three or more employed adults.

Table 39. Illness or injury over past 12 months by number of employed adults

Employed adults	% ill or injured
0	7%
1	10%
2	11%
3	9%
Total	9%

Table 40 suggests that, among those children reported to have suffered from illness or injury, the likelihood of consulting with a health worker increases with the number of employed adults. This could indicate the ability to pay fees, travel and other costs associated with seeking assistance.

Table 40. Consultation of ill and injured with health workers by number of employed adults

Number of employed adults	% consulting
0	83%
1	86%
2	89%
3	85%
Total	85%

Table 41 shows that expense is more likely to be given as a reason for not consulting with a health worker when children are ill or injured as the number of employed adults in the household decreases.

Table 41. Expense as a reason for not consulting by number of employed adults

Number of employed adults	% too expensive
0	26%
1	15%
2	12%
3	16%
Total	19%

Table 42 suggests (but with very small differences) that children living in households with no employed adults and those in households with three or more employed adults are more likely to access welfare services than those with one or two employed adults in the household. The pattern is positive in terms of welfare services targeting those children who are likely to need them most.

Table 42. Accessing welfare services by number of employed adults

Employed adults	% accessing welfare
0	3%
1	2%
2	1%
3	3%
Total	2%

Table 43 suggests that there is no relationship between the likelihood that a child will be disabled and the number of employed adults in the household. Overall, only 1% of children are reported to be disabled.

Table 43. Disability by number of employed adults

Employed adults	% disabled
0	1%
1	1%
2	1%
3	0%
Total	1%

ACCESS TO HOUSEHOLD SERVICES

The set of tables above compares the situation of children in households with varying numbers of employed adults. Table 44 focuses on households which include at least one child and compares the situation of households with varying numbers of employed adults in respect of access to various services and assets. The table suggests that the likelihood of the household having piped water on site and using electricity as the main fuel for cooking increases as the number of employed adults increases. The likelihood that a household owns books also increases as the number of employed adults increases.

Table 44. Access to services and assets by number of employed adults

	0 employed	1 employed	2 employed	3 employed	Total
Piped water on site	43%	68%	83%	78%	62%
Electricity for cooking	33%	59%	80%	71%	54%
Possession of books	60%	72%	83%	81%	70%

CONCLUSION

This chapter has, as expected, showed that the presence of employed adults in a household is likely to improve the wellbeing of children as measured along a range of axes. It has showed that children in different categories (race, age, etc) differ in the likelihood that they will have access to employed adults in this way. Further analysis would almost certainly reveal that the extent of the benefit would differ across groups, for example because of the different mean incomes of employed adults from different race groups. The discussion in respect of the impact of male vs. female earners points to the possibilities in this type of analysis.

The chapter has only scratched the surface of the possibilities for analysing the impact of access to employed adults for children. The possibilities in the existing data are far from exhausted. However, there are also many challenges. One challenge is the limited size of the database when one focuses on particular groups. A second challenge is the large number of confounding variables. Among these are the size of the household, the number of earners per resident, the sex and age of the earners, and the type and level of remuneration of the employment. Before spending long hours in complicated analysis, more thought is needed on which types of analysis will be most useful for informing policy rather than simply for academic interest.

REFERENCES

Budlender D., Chobokoane N. & Mpetsheni Y. 2001. *A Survey of Time Use: How South African women and men spend their time.* Cape Town: Statistics SA.

Commission on Gender Equality. March 2004. *Implementation of the Maintenance Act in the Magistrates' Courts.* Johannesburg: CGE.

Dorrington R. & Kramer S. 2004. *The 2004 mid-year estimates: Method, reliability and implications.* Centre for Actuarial Research seminar, University of Cape Town.

---

[1] In this and other tables the small numbers with sex and other defining characteristics unspecified are omitted from the disaggregated tables and rows but included in the totals.

[2] 18 (unweighted) of the resident mothers identified in the dataset were recorded as male and thus excluded from further analysis. A further 13 (unweighted) mothers could not be found at all in the database recording employment status.

[3] A dash indicates that the sample size is extremely small.

[4] Again, there are some errors in the database in that three (unweighted) of the identified fathers are female and 13 cannot be found at all in the dataset with information about labour market status.

CHAPTER 2

ADDRESSING CHILD RIGHTS AND CHILD LABOUR:
A POVERTY STRATEGY FOR SOUTH AFRICA?

KATERINA NICOLAOU AND MONET DURIEUX

INTRODUCTION

Children are the future of our country and they essentially rely on adults to nurture and take care of them. As a result, the South African Constitution, as the supreme law in the country, ensures that children, as citizens of the country, enjoy all the same rights as their fellow adult citizens. Those who are under the age of 18 are afforded special rights. Most government departments have special programmes to protect and maintain the rights of children, either directly or indirectly, and to comply with the Constitution.

Section 28 of the Constitution states that children under the age of 18 have a right to be protected from work that is: exploitative, hazardous or otherwise inappropriate for their age; detrimental to their schooling; and detrimental to their social, physical, mental, spiritual or moral development. Poverty is a significant cause of child labour; to assist their families and alleviate the hardships they face poor children are prepared to engage in more harmful and detrimental forms of child labour than would otherwise be the case. Under these conditions their families tend to condone or encourage such work. Structural factors underlie South Africa's poverty problem with the poor being predominantly African, female or members of female-headed households, situated primarily in the rural areas with limited access to land, education, assets and basic services. This can be attributed to the apartheid legacy. In South Africa, poverty is exacerbated by lack of employment opportunities, especially among the youth, and the HIV/AIDS pandemic which results in the death of breadwinners and economically active earners and imposes care-giving costs on households.

> Both long-term poverty and impoverishment must be addressed, as both encourage child labour. Further, both sets of factors interact, and those in chronic poverty are more vulnerable to conjunctural shocks. Structural factors underlying chronic poverty are generally addressed in broad national strategies on development and poverty reduction. In South Africa, grants, public works programmes, income-generating programmes, and job creation are among government's strategies to address income poverty (Department of Labour, 2003).

Since children from poorer households are more likely to spend more hours working than their wealthier counterparts, efforts to address child labour cannot be done in isolation from strategies that aim to promote employment among the adult population in South Africa.

This chapter will highlight some of government's efforts to promote the rights of the child and explain the Department of Labour's strategy that aims to eliminate child labour. Finally, the chapter will also address government's efforts to promote employment initiatives to assist both youth and adults, in an attempt to indirectly alleviate child labour.

POVERTY AND UNEMPLOYMENT IN SOUTH AFRICA: DRIVERS OF CHILD LABOUR

UNEMPLOYMENT

According to the March 2005 Labour Force Survey (LFS), official unemployment declined from 27.9% in March 2004 to 26.5% in March 2005. Although unemployment for Africans decreased from 34.2% in March 2004 to 31.6% in March 2005, unemployment for this race group is significantly higher than for any other group. Despite unemployment rates increasing for Indians/Asians, coloureds and whites for the same period, these groups have significantly lower rates, particularly among whites. Not surprisingly, unemployment for women is higher than their male counterparts and youth are over-represented in the unemployment rates.

The International Labour Organisation (ILO) estimates that in 2003 there were approximately 88 million unemployed young people, compared to 69.5 million in 1993. As many as 500 million youths[1] are expected to enter the labour market in the next decade. The President of the ILO Association in the Philippines, Gert Gus, said: "labour market-focused education and training is the key to prepare the youth to become more productive and to develop their talents". In addition, there should be equal access to education and more on-the-job and vocational-technical skills development programmes for enhancing the employability of the youth (Olarte, 2005). Youth in South Africa are defined as individuals between the ages of 15 and 34 years. According to the March 2005 LFS, there are approximately 17.4 million youth, using the South African definition. Furthermore, according to the survey, official unemployment for individuals aged 15 to 24 is 52.6% and for those aged 25 to 34 the rate is 31%. Table 1 below details youth unemployment.

Table 1: Youth unemployment by race (official rate)

Age group	Total population	Number unemployed	Race % of unemployed youths			
			African	Coloured	Asian	White
15-24	9 489 000	1 206 000	85.7	10.0	2.3	2.0
25-34	7 932 000	1 613 000	89.6	6.4	2.4	1.4

Source: Statistics SA – LFS March 2005

The percentage of youth that is discouraged work seekers is high in comparison to other age groups. The figure below shows the percentage of discouraged work seekers as a percentage of the working age population.

**Figure 1: Discouraged work seekers as a percentage of
the working age population**

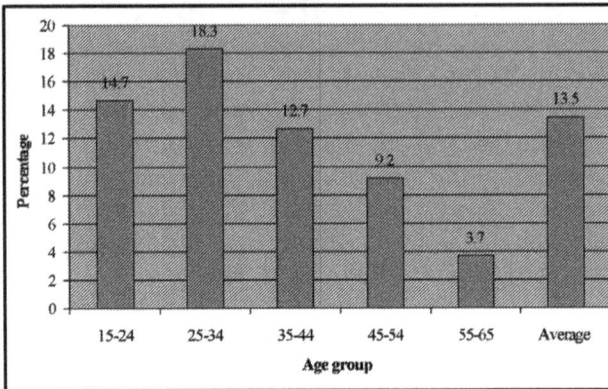

Source: Statistics SA – LFS September 2004

Labour force participation rates have remained somewhat stable and the labour absorption rate has increased marginally from 39.1% to 40.3% over the same period. Labour absorption for both males and females has increased over the period. Labour absorption rates are significantly lower for individuals aged 15 to 24 years of age, compared to those aged 35 to 54. In other words, less than 15% of the labour force aged 15 to 24 is employed compared to nearly 62% of those in the 35 to 44 age group. The table below highlights the absorption rates for the various age groups.

Table 2: Labour absorption rates per age group – March 2004 to March 2005

	15-24 years	25-34 years	35-44 years	45-54 years	55-65 years	RSA average
March 04	12.8	49.7	60.3	56.8	34.7	39.1
Sept 04	13.6	50.1	60.1	58.4	35.1	39.7
March 05	13.4	50.4	61.5	58.7	37.7	40.3

Source: Statistics SA – LFS March 2005

The March 2005 LFS shows that nearly 27% of the population cite the fact that they cannot find work as the reason for not being economically active. A further 37% are scholars with 11.6% being either disabled or ill.

Compared to March 2004, employment increased in March 2005 in Gauteng, KwaZulu-Natal, North West province and the Eastern Cape. Furthermore, significant gains in employment seem to be in the trade sector as well as in the community services sector. The severe drought in many parts of the country affected agricultural employment, with employment declining 16% from 1 258 000 in March 2004 to 1 063 000 in September 2004. This sector saw a marginal increase in numbers in March 2005 (ie 107 000 jobs). Furthermore, employment increased consistently in both the non-agricultural formal sector (3.6% or 267 000 jobs) as well as the non-agricultural informal sector (17.3% or 305 000 jobs) from March 2004 to March 2005.

LINKING POVERTY TO THE LABOUR MARKET, SPECIFICALLY CHILD LABOUR

Wage income is the most important source of household income in South Africa, representing more than 50% of household income in all households (UNDP South Africa, 2003: 74).

> *It is well recognised that employment is one of the most fundamental economic opportunities. It provides people with incomes that enable them to purchase a range of goods and services with which to enhance their and their dependants' standards of living...[E]mployment is the bridge between economic growth, poverty eradication and opportunities for human development (UNDP South Africa, 2003: 76).*

The February 2001 LFS shows that the first two income quintiles, representing the poorest households in South Africa, rely heavily on remittances and pension incomes. Moreover, more than 40% of the households in each quintile have no members working. Between 40 and 60% of the households in each of the second, third and fourth quintiles have only one household member working. This is most pronounced for African households, showing the importance of and dependence on income earners either through wage income, a pension or a grant. Sole earners supporting the poorest households are more likely to be in low skill, low paid and low quality occupations. Moreover, these jobs have very few benefits and are not very secure, raising the vulnerability of these households.

> *Thus the type of employment available to, or occupied by, the poor is an additional problem faced by the "working poor". Moreover, it reflects a labour market structure in which a relatively large number of households (with one or more workers) in the first income quintile are trapped in poverty (UNDP South Africa, 2003: 77).*

Given the dire circumstances facing the poor, it is not surprising that they allow their children to work in unsatisfactory conditions, compromising their physical, emotional, intellectual and spiritual development. Employers favour children as they are cheaper than their adult counterparts and rarely stand up for themselves.

CHILD LABOUR IN SOUTH AFRICA: SETTING THE SCENE

In 1999, the Department of Labour commissioned a household-based survey, conducted in all nine provinces and all settlement areas, known as the Survey of Activities of Young People (SAYP). In the first phase of the survey 26 081 households in 900 primary sampling units were selected and visited to ascertain whether there was at least one child between the ages of 5 and 17 in it who was involved in some form of child work. In the second phase, a sub-sample of the households containing at least one working child was selected and more detailed questions were asked of all the children. A total of 4 494 households were selected.

Defining "child labour" is not a simple exercise. The survey aimed to investigate what kind of activities children are involved in without passing judgement on what was labour or not and whether these were good or bad for the child. The survey aimed to cover all work-like activities. One set of questions asked whether the child had been involved in any form of activities for pay, profit or economic family gain in the past seven days or 12 months. Activities included: running any kind of business; helping in a family business; helping in farming activities; catching or gathering fish, prawns, shellfish, wild animals or any other food for sale or for family consumption; any work for a wage, salary or payment in kind; begging for food or money in public; fetching water or fuel; housekeeping or family care activities within households (household chores); and helping with cleaning and improvements at school unrelated to studies (school-related activities).

The SAYP estimated that there were 13.4 million children between the ages of 5 and 17. From the survey, 45% or six million children were undertaking at least one hour of "economic" work a week and/or five or more hours of school-related work and/or seven or more hours of household chores. Using a slightly higher cut-off, 12.5% or 1.7 million children were involved in 12 hours of economic activities a week and/or 12 hours of school labour and/or 14 hours of household chores.

Fetching fuel and water, deemed to be an economic activity according to the SAYP, is the most common economic activity that children are involved in. A total of 4.5 million children (or 33%) of all children aged 5 to 17 spend at least one hour or more on fetching fuel and water a week. Excluding the fetching of fuel and water and unpaid domestic work from the economic activities, 3% or 0.4 million children work for more than 12 hours a week. Boys are more likely to be involved in economic activities while girls are more likely to be involved in household chores and child-minding.

Of the children engaged in economic activities for three or more hours a week, 59% (or 625 000 children) stated that the reason they worked was because they had a duty to their family; 15% (or 155 000 children) stated that they worked to assist their family with money; and a further 16% (164 000) indicated that they worked for pocket money.

Older children are more likely to work than younger children. For the category of children working three or more hours a week, 5% (or 261 000) were 5 to 9 year olds, 9% (or 467 000) were 10 to 14 year olds and 15% (408 000) were aged 15 to 17, who are legally allowed to work.

According to the survey, 12% of children in deep rural areas are likely to work for three or more hours a week, with 11% of children being involved in commercial farming. Most children are not paid for their economic activities and are primarily involved in agriculture and trade which are likely to be micro enterprises. The table below highlights activities by industry.

Table 3: Children aged 5-14 working three hours per week or more in economic activities by industry

Industry	Number of children working		Proportion of these children who live in deep rural areas (%)		Number of children working as a proportion of all children aged 5-14 (%)	
	3 h/w +	12 h/w +	3 h/w +	12 h/w +	3 h/w +	12 h/w +
Subsistence agriculture	390 000	129 000	83	91	3.7	1.2
Wholesale and retail trade	225 000	86 000	58	63	2.1	0.8
Commercial agriculture	67 000	29 000	61	52	0.6	0.3
Manufacturing and construction	15 000	12 000	93	100	0.1	0.1
Private households	13 000	8 000	31	50	0.1	0.1
Total	728 000	266 000	44	77	6.8	2.5

Source: Department of Labour – Towards a National Child Labour Action Programme for South Africa: Discussion Document, October 2002, pg 20.

It is quite evident from the table above that a vast majority of the children who engage in economic activities – with the exception of private households – live in the deep rural areas. Furthermore, the SAYP also indicated that as the number of hours of work per week increases, so does the proportion of children working in all industries, except commercial agriculture, who live in rural areas. "This is probably related to the high levels of poverty in the deep rural areas, and indicates that these areas should be emphasised in a programme of action" (Department of Labour, 2002: 20). Children in households with an annual income of R4 200 or less account for 21% of all children. However, 26% of these children are engaged only in economic activities of three hours per week or more, while 28% of these are engaged in school labour only, 25% of these are involved in both economic and school labour and 27% are involved in economic, school and household activities. In contrast, households with an annual income of R18 000 account for 29% of all children. However only 18% are involved in economic, household and school work. Thus the problem of child labour really points to a problem of poverty and even unemployment.

Looking at the household composition, 39% of children in South Africa live with both parents, with 25% of these children collecting fuel. Moreover, 70% of the children who collect fuel and water live with their mother only or with neither parent. A small number of children engaged in begging were captured in the survey. Of these 15% lived with both parents while 61% lived with neither parent. Not surprisingly, only 9% of white children worked three or more hours a week compared to 41% of African children.

Children aged 5 to 14 years who are deemed to be working in contravention of the law account for more than 30% of working children. Moreover, 70% of children are working illegally work in family businesses. "While such children are assisting their family in 'carrying on' business – and as such are technically employed – it will often be very difficult to prove since both the family and the child are likely to deny this" (Department of Labour, 2002: 21).

Surprisingly, working did not seem to prevent children from attending school. However, 35% of children working between 43 and 49 hours were not attending school. These children are predominantly older children and are in full-time work. Nevertheless, work does interfere with the school performance of children, thus contributing to poor education outcomes. These children had less time to devote to studying and experienced difficulties in catching up, compared to children who were not involved in any work activity.[2]

Using the narrow definition of economic activity for children working three hours per week or more, 61% (or 2.1 million children) said that they were exposed to hazardous conditions, 2% (or 58 000) suffered illness related to their work and 4% (or 153 000) said that they had been injured at work. The ILO's Worst Forms of Child Labour Convention of 1999 identifies several types of child labour that must be addressed as a priority by ratifying states:

• All forms of slavery or practices similar to slavery;
• The use, procuring or offering of a child for prostitution, for the production of pornography or for pornographic performances;
• The use, procuring or offering of a child for illicit activities, in particular for the production and trafficking of drugs;
• Work which by its nature or circumstances is likely to harm the health, safety or morals of children ("hazardous work").

Very little information was available from the 1999 SAYP on the worst forms of child labour, except for some forms of hazardous work. Some evidence on the worst forms of child labour can be derived from some of the non-government organisations (NGOs) that work in these areas. However, the evidence is sporadic and compiled on a case-by-case basis.

Child labour seems to occur in poorer households that have limited access to resources and income. These are essentially households located in the former home-land areas and are thus predominantly African. Lack of access to services such as piped water and electricity raise the likelihood of children fetching and carrying heavy loads of wood and water. Service deprivation is a good proxy for measuring poverty. Moreover, the "importance of poverty as a factor encouraging child work is confirmed by the responses of many children that their reason for working is to contribute to the family" (Department of Labour, 2002: 29).

To get a better understanding of the current status of child labour in South Africa, it is critical that a follow-up survey be undertaken. Numbers need to be updated to get a sense of whether the child labour situation is improving or deteriorating and whether there have been shifts in the predominance in specific sectors or not. Without this information, it is very difficult to make informed policy decisions to alleviate child labour.

Having set the scene regarding child labour in South Africa, the next section highlights the legislation that is geared to promote the general rights of the child.

THE RIGHTS OF THE CHILD IN SOUTH AFRICA

South Africa has a very progressive Constitution that provides special rights to children under the age of 18 and sets the foundation for government policies and strategies that benefit children. As a result, South Africa has developed numerous pieces of legislation that, either entirely or in part, specifically address the rights of children. Moreover, South Africa has also ratified a series of charters and conventions that offer special protection to children. It would be impossible to address each of these in adequate detail. This section merely addresses some of the key legislation that broadly targets children, with special emphasis on child labour.

THE SOUTH AFRICAN CONSTITUTION

Children, as citizens of the country, enjoy all the same rights as adult citizens, but the Constitution also gives children under the age of 18 special rights. The following items in the Bill of Rights within the Constitution relate to children's rights:[3]

- Every child has the right to family or parental care, or to appropriate alternative care when removed from the family environment;
- Every child has the right to a name and nationality from birth;
- Every child has the right to basic nutrition, shelter, basic healthcare services and social services;
- Every child has the right to be protected from maltreatment, neglect, abuse or degradation;
- Everyone has the right to freedom and security of the person, which includes the right to be free from all forms of violence from either public or private sources;
- Every child has the right to be protected from exploitative labour practices;
- Every child has the right to have a legal practitioner assigned to the child by the state and at state expense in civil proceedings affecting the child, if substantial injustice would otherwise result;
- Every child has the right not to be detained except as a measure of last resort;
- A child's best interests are of paramount importance in every matter concerning the child;
- Everyone has the right to basic education (early childhood development);
- The rights of children with disabilities are protected in terms of article 23 of the United Nations Convention on the Rights of the Child (CRC).
- The rights of refugee and foreign unaccompanied children are protected in terms of article 22 of the CRC.

OTHER GOVERNMENT INITIATIVES

Initiatives by government that aim to address the rights of the child can also be found in the following legislation:

- The Child Rights Framework, as developed by the Presidency;
- The Basic Conditions of Employment Act (BCEA) that prohibits children below the age of 15 from taking up employment. Children from the ages of 15 to 17 are permitted to take up employment, but not if that work is detrimental to their develop-

ment. The necessary safety precautions need to be taken;
- Amendments to the Sexual Offences Act and Sexual Offenders Bill address the commercial sexual exploitation of children;
- The Child Justice Bill;
- The South African Schools Act states that no one may prevent a child from attending school;
- The Child Care Act includes the provision of social services and social grants in addition to prohibiting the abuse of children;
- The Children's Bill addresses the rights of children more comprehensively and governs every possible area of engagement (thus overlapping with all the above legislation).

CONVENTIONS RATIFIED

South Africa has ratified a number of conventions relating to children, including the following:

- The CRC of 1989 provides that every child has a right to be protected from economic exploitation and from any work that is likely to be hazardous or interfere with the child's education, or deemed to be harmful to the child's health or physical, mental, spiritual, moral or social development. However, the convention does not set a minimum age, but refers to other international instruments. The convention says that the best interests of the child must be a primary consideration in all actions affecting children, whether undertaken by government or private actors;
- The African Charter on the Rights and Welfare of the Child of 1990 provides that children should be protected from economic exploitation in addition to stating that children have responsibilities towards their families, societies, communities and the international community;
- The ILO Minimum Age Convention of 1973 provides that children under the age of 15 should only engage in economic activities if they are over the age of 12 and the work is light and unlikely to harm their health, development and schooling. Moreover, the minimum age for work that is likely to jeopardise health, safety or morals is 18;
- The ILO Worst Forms of Child Labour Convention of 1999 requires ratifying governments to take measures to abolish the worst forms of child labour, which include slavery, child prostitution, using a child in illegal activities and hazardous work that is likely to harm the child's health, safety or morals. Each country should determine "hazardous work" in consultation with employer and worker organisations.

Thus, there are numerous efforts to address and protect the rights of the child in South Africa, which are guided by the South African Constitution. Annexure A is a scorecard of government expenditure on several programmes that relate to children.[4] In the following section, the focus will be primarily on government's key strategy developed by the Department of Labour to address child labour.

ADDRESSING CHILD LABOUR IN SOUTH AFRICA: THE DEPARTMENT OF LABOUR'S CHILD LABOUR ACTION PROGRAMME

The South African government has embarked on a process of developing an appropriate National Action Programme to address child labour. The Department of Labour is the lead institution in this regard. Like all other policies, bills and legislation, the starting point is always the Constitution. The Child Labour Action Programme (CLAP) derives its mandate from section 28 of the Constitution that states that children under the age of 18 have a right to be protected from work that is:

• Exploitative, hazardous or otherwise inappropriate for their age;
• Detrimental to their schooling; or
• Detrimental to their social, physical, mental, spiritual or moral development.

The CLAP does not only consider "work" to be economic activities in the form of employment, but includes activities in the form of household chores such as the collection of wood or water when they are exploitative, hazardous, inappropriate for their age or detrimental to their schooling or development. Thus, according to the CLAP "child labour" includes all forms of work that is detrimental to the child.

THE CLAP PROCESS

To develop an action programme to assist working children in South Africa, it was necessary to understand the extent of the problem. Thus, a credible database on child labour was necessary. A preliminary investigation was undertaken in 1996 to determine the appropriate tool, with a national household-based survey being recommended. In 1999, Statistics South Africa conducted the first national survey on child activities, the SAYP. The survey, as well as the policy development process that followed, was conducted with financial and other support from the ILO. The result was an official discussion document released in October 2002 entitled "Towards a National Child Labour Action Programme for South Africa". Furthermore, all qualitative research related to this topic available from various sources in South Africa was also analysed. Using these two critical processes, the Department of Labour began a series of consultation processes with the South African public, both adults and children. Stemming from the inputs from these processes, the Department of Labour, together with a core team of sector experts and the ILO, engaged with key stakeholders, including all government departments, on the proposed action steps necessary to alleviate child labour.

Stakeholders indicated whether they supported the proposed action step that affected them and engaged in a process of refining the steps. The Programme of Action was updated to incorporate the action steps that various line function departments were already engaged in. Stakeholders also agreed to commitments of financial and human resources. Furthermore, line function departments agreed to seek and motivate for additional funding where necessary to initiate or implement the action steps. The process also highlighted which steps were urgent and possible to undertake in the short term and others that were desirable but had massive financial and political ramifications. The consultative process ended with the drafting of a CLAP document for South Africa, which was accepted by all relevant

35

departments in 2003. This document describes 131 actions steps, separated out for each department.

Currently, the costs of the CLAP are being assessed (ie the financial implications of each action per department) and the programme is being presented to Cabinet for noting and preliminary approval.

A BRIEF LOOK AT THE CLAP

Many government programmes are aimed at alleviating poverty, such as the child support grant, school nutrition programmes, free basic healthcare and so forth. The CLAP is designed to complement existing government programmes while simultaneously addressing child labour.

In developing the CLAP, care was taken to support existing initiatives and avoid duplication. When assessing the programme in its entirety, including all possible proposed action steps, the CLAP is in actual fact a poverty strategy for South Africa. This has massive financial ramifications for the fiscus.

This section will highlight some aspects of the CLAP. It will not attempt a complete assessment of the programme or a summary. Harmful work activities need to be identified by the programme. The policy aims to address the following work activities that increase or cause potential harm to children:

- Long hours;
- Night work;
- Work that exposes the child to:
  - o dangerous circumstances, tools, chemicals;
  - o commercial sexual exploitation;
  - o high strain, heavy loads or exhausting work;
  - o illegal work;
  - o ergonomically unsuitable work;
  - o excessive responsibility;
  - o repetitive or non-stimulating work;
- Work that is detrimental to schooling;
- Work that is degrading and undermines the child's self-worth;
- Work that reduces the time for recreation and rest;
- Work where adults coerce or intimidate the child, restrict the child's movements unreasonably or where there is no caring adult present; and
- Work that is performed on the street or work that is hidden, isolated or not easily monitored.

The categories below are not deemed to be child labour but they are included in the Programme of Action as areas that need special action since they are detrimental to the child's overall wellbeing:

- Fetching water and fuel;
- Commercial sexual exploitation (which is a crime);
- Inappropriate levels of domestic chores;
- Indirect forms of exploitation;
- Inadequate child care facilities.

Furthermore, the programme identifies certain circumstances and characteristics that render children more vulnerable. These are age, gender and violence.

To try to address poverty and impoverishment, the programme identifies the elimination of illiteracy, improving access to free and quality basic education for all and the social or welfare grants as critical. The CLAP emphasises job creation for adults as a means of addressing poverty, unemployment and therefore child labour. The CLAP states:

> *The biggest opportunities for income-earning opportunities are the public works programmes. Income-generating projects could make a small contribution. The Basic Conditions of Employment Act's blanket prohibition on employment of children should also encourage jobs for adults...*
> *[T]he following is proposed:*
>
> *(2) One of the factors of deciding where to implement public works programmes should be in areas where many children are involved in the worst forms of child labour...Lead institution: Department of Public Works; Secondary institution: Department of Labour. New policy: Elaboration of existing policy. Once-off cost: minimal. Recurrent cost: minimal. Time line: To be introduced within one year of adoption of policy.*
>
> *(3) Assessing the government's job creation policy to ensure that jobs created go to adults and not children. Lead institution: Department of Trade and Industry; Secondary institution: Department of Labour. New policy: Elaboration of existing policy. Once-off cost: nil. Recurrent cost: minimal. Time line: To be introduced within one year of adoption of policy (Department of Labour, 2005).*

All the 131 action steps are developed in exactly the same way as the above policy proposal. The Departments of Labour, Social Development, Justice and Education have the most action steps. However there are action steps for all departments since all can contribute towards alleviating child labour, directly or indirectly. These are some of the steps that have been identified for the Department of Labour:

- The provisions of the BCEA on child labour are too narrowly defined;
- Regulations regarding children aged 15 to 17 need to be drafted to guide employers on what work is acceptable;
- The law should require child workers to be paid at the same rate as adults;
- Labour inspectors should receive training on how to address child labour;
- Resources must be allocated to ensure the enforcement of child labour provisions;
- National awareness campaigns must be undertaken and developed, including the BCEA provisions relating to "forced labour", provisions on the trafficking of children, children involved in making and selling liquor; the disadvantages and dangers of adult work that encourages child labour; and
- Sectors that have child labour as defined in the policy must be monitored and inspected.

The Department of Social Development's action steps include some of the following:

- Poverty alleviation initiatives, including the rollout of grants, should be targeted at child labour;
- Extension of the child support grant up to the end of the school year in which the child turns 15;
- In the medium term, the extension of the child support grant to those aged 16 and 17;
- Addressing the birth certificate and identification document problem with respect to the child support grant, especially for caregivers in poorer and rural areas;
- Appropriate strategies should be found for providing childcare facilities, especially in sectors and areas where children often have to look after their younger siblings, with a focus on the rural poor.

The CLAP highlights steps that in many instances are already being undertaken in the various departments, although in some cases the programme needs additional resources to be scaled up. There are several action steps, however, that have both political and financial implications. An example of this is the medium term proposal to extend the child support grant to children aged 15, 16 and 17. This proposal is extremely costly and would require political buy-in as well.

THE INTER-DEPARTMENTAL CLAP COMMITTEE

The implementation of the CLAP is overseen by an interdepartmental Child Labour Action Programme Implementation Committee (CLAPIC). The members of this committee come from key government departments, organised labour and business, NGOs and civil society, and the committee meets on a regular basis to ensure the implementation, monitoring and evaluation of the CLAP. Progress with regards to CLAP action steps, policy development and special projects on the worst forms of child labour are also reported on.

TOWARDS THE ELIMINATION OF THE WORST FORMS OF CHILD LABOUR

Towards the Elimination of the Worst Forms of Child Labour (TECL) is a programme initiated and funded by the ILO. TECL is a tool to assist member states to fulfil their obligations in terms of the Worst Forms of Child Labour Convention within a defined period of time. TECL essentially supports the CLAP initiative in addition to behaving as an executing agency for some of the key aspects relating to the CLAP. The TECL programme focuses on 45 action steps within the CLAP document. The key role players in this process are: the Department of Justice and Constitutional Development, in relation to the Child Justice Bill; the South African Police Services, assisting in investigations that will lead to the prosecution of those involved in criminal or illegal activities involving children; the Department of Education, assisting in identifying children needing assistance; the Department of Social Development, in terms of social grants; and the Department of Labour as the lead department with a supporting role played by a number of other government departments and NGOs.

The timeframe for this programme is three years. It began in April 2004 and has a budget of US$5 million, with supporting work done in Botswana, Lesotho, Namibia and Swaziland as well as in the sub-region. There are various projects within the TECL programme, including raising awareness around child labour issues, focusing on:

- Access to education;
- The prevalence of the worst forms of child labour;
- The negative impact of child labour; and
- Steps to take when encountering incidents of child labour, where such activities are detrimental to the child.

Furthermore, the TECL identifies four categories of the worst forms of labour: bonded labour; commercial sexual exploitation; trafficking of children ie children recruited to work far away from their homes and families; and the use of children in other illegal activities such as drug trafficking.

The TECL is currently piloting three projects with the aim of preventing children from participating in the worst forms of child labour, withdrawing and rehabilitating children already engaged in the worst forms of child labour and protecting children of working age from hazardous and dangerous working conditions. These are:

- Children Used By Adults to Commit Crimes (CUBAC). Very little is know about how children are used in criminal activities and NGOs have played a critical role in designing this pilot programme to help children who depend on and are involved with adult criminals in illegal activities, especially production or trafficking of drugs;
- Commercial Sexual Exploitation of Children (CSEC);
- The delivery of water to households that are far from safe sources of water.

The TECL programme is also responsible for monitoring the implementation of the CLAP. A sister programme to TECL, Reducing Exploitative Child Labour in Southern Africa (RECLISA), reports directly to the United States Education Initiative, and focuses on educational and social services.

ADDITIONAL DEPARTMENT OF LABOUR PROJECTS RELATING TO CHILDREN

Further interventions by the Department of Labour include the Sectoral Determinations for Children in the Performing Arts, launched on 29 July 2005, which enables the department to regulate the working conditions of children employed in this sector. Approval for employers wishing to engage children in this sector would be subject to the completion of a permit that would be evaluated according to the provision of article 8 of ILO Convention 182. This sectoral determination would also contribute to obtaining data on children in the performing arts, as inspections can be undertaken and appropriate remedial action taken.

The National Skills Development Strategy (NSDS) was launched by the Minister of Labour in February 2001, with key deliverables to be achieved by March 2005. In March 2005, the Minister launched the updated NSDS II, effective from 1 April 2005 to 31 March 2010. NSDS II has five key objectives and 20 success indicators, several of which relate to learnerships. There is no minimum age for learnerships, but since children up to the age of 15 are subject to compulsory schooling, learnerships are likely to start from age 15 onwards. The Act provides an institutional framework for a national strategy to develop and improve the skills of the South African workforce. However, it would be better if these programmes encouraged children under the age of 18 to complete school, even in the Further Education and Training (FET) sector, and then move onto learnership programmes that result in qualifications coupled with work-based training. Adults, especially those who have been unemployed for long periods, should be given preference.

Objective 1 of NSDS II refers to "prioritising and communicating critical skills for sustainable growth, development and equity". To achieve this, Success Indicator 1.2 requires information on critical skills to be made widely available to learners. The Department of Labour will be responsible for consolidating inputs from Sector Education and Training Authorities (SETAs) into a document that will highlight trends in employment, shortages in various occupational categories, and so forth. This information will be distributed widely to schools and FET colleges to guide learners on the needs of the labour market and inform their career decisions.

Thus the Department of Labour addresses the issue of child labour through a series of policies and legislative measures, including the BCEA, Sectoral Determinations for Children in the Performing Arts and the CLAP. However, the way to minimise child labour is to promote employment for youth[5] aged 18 and older who have left school as well as for the adult population.

GOVERNMENT PROGRAMMES FOR ALLEVIATING YOUTH AND ADULT UNEMPLOYMENT

Government does not have one strategic policy document targeting unemployment. Most government departments have policies or strategies that target the unemployed, either directly or indirectly. This section will give a brief overview of some of the government's key initiatives that aim to address unemployment. In addressing the youth and adult unemployment problem government has developed several programmes to promote: training and work-based experience; entrepreneurship through various mechanisms that assist small and micro enterprises; subsidised employment schemes such as the Expanded Public Works Programme (EPWP) that create either short-term or long-term employment; and legislative tax and levy breaks to small and medium enterprise learnership programmes.

THE NATIONAL SKILLS DEVELOPMENT STRATEGY

To address skills shortages and help reduce unemployment, the Ministers of Labour and Education jointly launched the Human Resources Development Strategy in 2001, which encompasses the National Skills Development Strategy. The Department of Education is responsible for human resource development, specifically early child-hood development, schooling, the FET colleges and tertiary education, while skills development refers to the role played by the Department of Labour with work-based training and development. The Human Resources Development Strategy comprises four pillars:

• A Demand pillar that endeavours to increase employer participation in life-long learning;

- A Supply pillar that improves the supply of high-quality skills;
- A Building the Base pillar that aims to improve the foundations for human development; and
- A Growing the Future pillar that promotes national capacity for innovation, research and development.

The major challenge facing government in the second decade of democracy is the quantity, quality and relevance of the skills being produced in South Africa. Strategic priorities include:

- Strengthening high-quality scarce skills;
- Strengthening the education base through early childhood learning and the schooling systems, with special emphasis on language, maths and science skills;
- Improving the pace and performance of service delivery post-schooling, which involves the successful transition to work by school leavers, and targets school drop outs and higher education graduates;
- Targeting learning strategies at the "second economy";
- Building the capacity of the state.

The Skills Development Act (1998) and the Skills Development Levies Act (1999) seek to address the work and training component of the Human Resources Development Strategy by fostering links between the Demand and Supply pillars, while preparing learners for employment and creating closer links between the employer and the employee. These objectives are achieved through a set of institutions – the SETAs – and incentives to employers to encourage and support training across all sectors of the economy. The Skills Development Levies Act requires that employers contribute 1% of their payroll to promote skills development and work-based training of both the employed and unemployed in the South African labour market. Payments are made to the South African Revenue Service, which then transfers 80% of this levy to the relevant SETA (that the employer has registered with). The remaining 20% is transferred to the National Skills Fund. A schematic representation of the levy is provided in Annexure B. The National Skills Development Strategy was launched in February 2001 for five years. A review undertaken in 2004 resulted in the strategy being updated and extended to 2010.

The SETAs were developed to promote skills development across 23 sectors of the economy by promoting learnerships. A learnership is a vocational and educational training programme, which combines theory and practise and that culminates in the learner obtaining a qualification that is registered with the National Qualifications Framework (NQF). In selecting participants for a learnership, government has agreed that 85% of learners must be black, 54% women and 4% should be people with disabilities. The focus of the learnership is on:

- Enabling the learner to use the skills that he/she has been taught;
- Teaching the learner why and how things are done;
- Assessing learners at various stages;
- Developing learnerships in areas where there is a skills shortage;
- Making learnerships available for young as well as more mature students, unlike apprenticeships that tend to be for young people starting their working lives.

41

Large and small employers enter into a learnership agreement with the leaner and a training provider. The SETAs approve every learnership programme before it can be forwarded to the Department of Labour and facilitate the funding of the learnership by disbursing mandatory grants on the receipt of workplace skills plans and implementation reports from employers. A learnership tax deduction has been provided to encourage companies to take on learners. Employers are entitled to claim the incentive twice, at the inception of the learnership and when the learnership is successfully concluded. The inception deduction is 70% of the learner's annual salary to a maximum of R17 500 if the learner is a current employee or R25 000 if the learner is not an employee and was unemployed. On completion of the learnership, the employer is entitled to deduct 100% of the annual salary subject to a maximum of R17 500 for existing employees and R25 000 for a previously unemployed learner. Employment and Skills and Development Lead Agencies (ESDLAs) have been established to reduce the administrative burden of learnerships on companies. They can assist companies to access grants, find the right candidates, conduct training, assess the competency of the learner and facilitate his or her certification. The length of a learnership programme differs, but is normally not less than one year.

The Departments of Education and Labour have gone to great lengths to align their policies. The NSDS II has several indicators that promote centres of excellence, thus allowing public providers and especially the FET sector to access SETA funds. Moreover, the recapitalisation of the FET sector is aimed at making this sector more responsive to labour market trends and the changing needs of the economy as well as to ensure private sector buy-in in the form of financial assistance and expertise. The NSDS II focuses on the quality and appropriateness of skills obtained by graduates in an effort to prevent a mismatch of the skills of graduates and the skills required by the economy, thereby promoting employment.

THE UMSOBOMVU YOUTH FUND
The Umsobomvu Youth Fund (UYF) was established in January 2001 to facilitate job creation and skills development among the youth of South Africa (ages 18-35). The three focus areas of the UYF are:

• Contact information and counselling;
• Skills development and transfer;
• Youth entrepreneurship programme.

The UYF supports the development of entrepreneurs in addition to promoting skills development projects for the youth through the FET colleges. The UYF has committed R22.3 million to 19 FET colleges for the creation of skills programmes and learnerships aimed at addressing skills shortages and youth unemployment. The projects will focus on bridging the gap between school and work

THE EXPANDED PUBLIC WORKS PROGRAMMES
The EPWP is a central element of government's commitment to the Growth and Development Summit (GDS). The EPWP is a framework that focuses on providing poverty and income relief through temporary work for the unemployed to carry out socially useful activities. The EPWP has been designed to provide participants with training and work experience that should enhance their ability to earn a living in

the future. The programme creates employment opportunities in the following sectors:

- **Infrastructure:** The creation of labour-intensive government-funded infrastructure projects managed by the Department of Public Works;
- **Environment and culture:** Projects in the public environmental programmes, such as Working for Water, under the leadership of the Department of Environmental Affairs and Tourism;
- **Social services:** Public social programmes such as Early Childhood Development and Home-Based Community Care Work where the Department of Social Development is the lead department;
- **Economics services:** Small enterprise learnerships (known as New Venture Creation learnerships) and incubation programmes under the Department of Trade and Industry.

Although the employment programmes in the infrastructure pillar provide short-term poverty relief and employment, the programmes within the social services pillar have the potential to provide more long-term relief. Since employment in the infrastructure sector is short-term, averaging about three months, additional exit strategies need to be considered where individuals can progress into second tier learnerships that can help build business enterprise skills, small business development, financial management and New Venture programmes.

The EPWP is integrated into the country's skills development strategy to ensure that participants acquire the skills needed by prevailing economic conditions. For example, the infrastructure or construction element of the EPWP has developed the necessary links with the construction SETA to provide training in the form of life skills.

The infrastructure component of the EPWP is facilitated through the Provincial and Municipal Infrastructure Grants, which include labour-intensive methods for building roads, schools, clinics and water infrastructure. Over the 2005/06 Medium Term Expenditure Framework period provincial and municipal infrastructure allocations amounted to R38.6 billion. These projects show the government's commitment to labour-intensive construction methods. According to the 2004 Budget, R4 billion will be allocated to the environmental and cultural sector for the period 2004/05 to 2008/09 and R600 million to the social sector for the same period.

THE NATIONAL YOUTH SERVICE
The National Youth Service (NYS) programme is an initiative coordinated by a committee comprising the National Youth Commission (NYC), the UYF, the South African Youth Council (SAYC), the National Departments of Labour and Education as well as other relevant departments.

The aim of this programme is to harness the potential of young people and improve their employability. Young people are trained in technical skills, which they can then put into practise at a community level. Moreover, there is a focus on providing life skills and developing a career path. A key element of the NYS programme is the integration of different programme components and coordination among the multiple programme partners.

YOUTH ADVISORY CENTRES

The Youth Advisory Centres (YACs) are funded through the UYF and implemented by NGOs. They provide information and counselling services to the youth and are located within communities. YACs are also a source of information on careers and job opportunities for youth, and services such as curriculum vitae writing, interview skills and life skills are provided.

The success of initiatives aimed at assisting the youth should include the following:

• Involving as many stakeholders as possible;
• Young people should be consulted in the design and implementation of a project;
• The projects must demonstrate sustainability;
• Quality standards should be met.

In conclusion, the discussion above highlights several programmes that government has in place to assist unemployed youth and adults. This discussion has excluded the efforts of the Department of Trade and Industry to promote Small, Micro and Medium Enterprises (SMMEs) and entrepreneurs either financially or technically; tax breaks for SMMEs; agricultural and land restitution programmes; social grant programmes that alleviate poverty; and a number of other programmes of various departments that promote employment by addressing critical skills needs through skills development and training programmes.

OVERLAPS IN GOVERNMENT POLICIES RELATING TO CHILDREN

The Office on the Rights of the Child (ORC) (also known as the Office on the Status of Children) in the Presidency is the central coordinating body within government on issues relating to children and its Child Rights Framework forms the overarching policy into which all other policies and legislation are integrated.

The Inter-Ministerial Core Group (IMC) and the National Programme of Action Steering Committee (NPASC) established by government is tasked with coordinating policies and legislation around child rights. The IMC comprised a number of ministers and their departments that had a key role to play in children's issues. This group was however dismantled and replaced by the National Plan of Action (NPA) that reports directly to Cabinet through the Social Cluster. The NPA's coordination resides in the ORC, located in the Presidency. The key functions of the NPA are:

• Co-ordinating policy development;
• Monitoring implementation of the policy developed;
• Evaluation of programmes developed for children.

The vision of the NPA is to create and build an environment where children are nurtured and can grow to their full potential. It also seeks to create a situation where children are given priority in their school, home and community life.

The above-mentioned legislation and policies on children are all interlinked and ultimately serve the same purpose, ie protecting one of the vulnerable groups within society, namely children, as well as outlining their rights.

The various committees that constitute the same government departments empha-
sise the overlaps within these programmes. Although the aim within government is
to ensure better coordination between government departments on matters that are
crosscutting, this is not always the case.

Moreover, it is more difficult to ensure that there is no duplication of work. For
example, the CLAP and the Children's Bill address issues relating to child labour, the
commercial sexual exploitation of children, child trafficking, and so forth. If departments do not work closely together, duplication is inevitable.

POLICY GAPS AND COORDINATION WEAKNESSES

It is clear that to reduce child labour it is critical to address unemployment and
poverty. There is a host of government programmes that target poverty and/or
unemployment. However, many of these programmes are uncoordinated, sporadic or
small scale and are therefore not able to make a significant difference to the people
plagued by poverty and unemployment. Although the Departments of Education
and Labour are working in a more coordinated manner, there are still great strides
that need to be taken to promote greater cohesion of policies to address skills
development as per the market's needs, thus promoting employment. These efforts
need to be complemented by the programmes of the Departments of Science and
Technology and Trade and Industry. Furthermore, a second tier of policies needs to
be coordinated relating to the policies of the Departments of Agriculture, Social
Development and Home Affairs. In assessing the type of coordination necessary to
unblock the bottlenecks that hamper employment creation and poverty alleviation,
it is evident that more and more role players are needed and this eventually becomes
a mammoth and very complex process, which is difficult to coordinate and manage.

The problem is often exacerbated by the low level of support for programmes where
junior officials attend committee meetings or key processes geared to promoting
coordination. Moreover, there is a lack of staff permanence and consistency in the
officials participating in these processes, resulting in coordination weaknesses. Junior
officials lack the vision necessary and cannot take decisions, thus stalling the process
and delaying the outcomes. Political buy-in is difficult to secure without continuous
engagement. However, one easy step to promoting greater coordination is simple
information sharing of processes and issues being addressed by various government
departments. A database should be developed containing information on the
projects of specific departments, contact details of the person responsible for the
programme as well as their area of speciality within the arena of children's issues.

Another means to promote coordination is an audit of all the policies and legislation
currently undertaken in departments so that further work could start from a common point of departure. Research should be conducted into how, in practice,
further coordination between stakeholders could be established, focusing on inter-
departmental committees and strengthening the capacity at the ORC within the
Presidency to help it in its role as overall coordinator of all children's issues.

Promoting coordination between government departments is already quite complex.
To succeed, coordination between government and civil society in some kind of part-

nership is critical to ensure the most efficient development of policies and pro-grammes that affect children and their unemployed and/or poor parents.

The CLAP is an excellent example of a strategy that requires greater coordination between government departments and civil society. The Department of Labour and the ILO team have devoted a lot of time and attention to greater coordination between government departments, civil society and NGOs. Yet it has been a cumber-some and difficult exercise, although the effort to include civil society and NGOs proved to be useful and informative in developing policies and programmes in the CLAP and the TECL programmes.

As mentioned above, the CLAP is a poverty strategy, although its primary focus is child labour. Future enforcement of child labour restrictions will render families worse off financially. Although the CLAP does highlight employment programmes such as the EPWP, and indicates that these are necessary to alleviate child labour, these are not the salient elements of the CLAP. Where a child is taken out of work, especially if no adults are working, there needs to be a referral system between gov-ernment departments that will enable the family to receive a child support grant. Alternatively they must be given preference in the EPWP programmes or helped to enter a learnership or skills development programme through the National Skills Development Strategy, or a New Venture Creation Programme through the Department of Trade and Industry and the Department of Labour or participate in or receive financial and technical support through the Department of Trade and Industry's SMME initiatives, or receive financial and other support through the UYF, and so forth.

There is no central processing centre that assesses the needs of the individual in an holistic and consistent manner. Currently, adults have to link up with the various government programmes by themselves, and lack of finance might render this impossible. This is the most critical policy gap and coordination weakness of govern-ment. Despite the CLAP being a poverty strategy, when it comes to enforcement it could in fact exacerbate poverty and worsen the conditions and environment that children live in. It is quite probable that abuse towards children will worsen as adults or parents resent the added burden placed on them by the child. Greater initiatives are necessary to promote the referral linkages in government otherwise there will be unintended consequences of certain policy actions.

Another referral failure relates more directly to children between 15 and 17 years old who are either committing crimes on behalf of adults or are being commercially sex-ually exploited. Although children can be referred to relevant safe houses, if policies are not in place to address their long-term needs by either training them or placing them in meaningful employment where they can support themselves, the child will re-enter the abusive environment when released from the safe house. This is another prominent coordination weakness and policy gap that applies more generally to poli-cies in place that assist children.

Recent amendments in the Treasury Guidelines for the 2006 Medium Term Expenditure Process emphasised improved synchronisation of cross-cutting issues between government departments. Several cross-cutting issues were piloted by the

National Treasury in an effort to promote "joined up government" discussions and policy debates. Success in the pilots will allow this to become a prominent feature of the process in years to come. The discussions will highlight duplication as well as coordination weaknesses and future engagement, while the appropriate placement of funds will allow departments to work more closely together. Thus in future the budget process will force greater coordination between departments.

CONCLUSION

The South African Constitution protects the rights of the child in an effort to secure the optimal development of future generations in this country. Several government policies and programmes have been developed stemming from the South African Constitution. Initiatives are geared to ensure good quality education, access to adequate nutrition, income supplementation for primary care-givers, access to basic services and infrastructure, access to social assistance and measures that prevent the child from engaging in activities that will hamper his or her mental, emotional, physical and spiritual development. One such activity relates to children under the age of 15 engaging in child labour.

Children from poorer households, especially in rural areas, are more likely to engage in child labour. Children between the ages of 15 and 17 leave school in search of work to assist their families financially at the cost of their own development. Thus, there is a clear link between unemployment and poverty and child labour. Addressing poverty and unemployment contributes towards the alleviation of child labour.

Government has developed several pieces of legislation and ratified several charters in an effort to promote the rights of the child in South Africa. The Child Labour Action Programme or CLAP is a strategy that addresses all forms of child labour. It coordinates the efforts of all relevant government departments by incorporating what they are already doing in a systematic and consistent manner. Much of the CLAP refers to existing government programmes. However, it also refers to programmes that can be extended or scaled up in the medium to long term. The CLAP also includes programmes that aim to alleviate unemployment.

Government has several initiatives that target the unemployed and aim to reduce poverty. These include SMME support through the Department of Trade and Industry's financial and technical support initiatives; tax breaks for SMMEs; EPWP opportunities; the National Skills Development Strategy and New Venture Creation initiatives; UYF programmes and other programmes that target the youth; support to subsistence agriculture farmers; social assistance; and free basic services.

However, although all government departments have programmes that endeavour to promote employment and/or alleviate poverty, government's efforts are not coordinated into a consistent poverty or unemployment strategy. Possibly the most prominent government weakness centres on the uncoordinated manner in which these various programmes interact and engage with each other.

Enforcement of the CLAP will exacerbate poverty, especially if there is poor coordination between government departments in referring and placing the adult parents of the child into meaningful work through the various government employment initiatives. Another policy gap centres on the long-term wellbeing of the child because enforcement programmes that place the child in places of safety are only short-term measures, with the child having to return to the home environment or having nowhere to go after leaving the place of safety. The referrals after leaving the places of safety are left up to NGOs, which have limited financial resources.

As the CLAP starts to move towards its implementation phase, coordination will become more critical. The 2006 MTEF process piloted several cluster discussions quite successfully, implying that issues around children will feature more prominently next year and in years to come. Thus, in the future, the budget process will drive greater coordination between government departments.

ANNEXURE A: GOVERNMENT'S SCORE CARD REGARDING EXPENDITURE AND ACHIEVEMENTS RELATING TO CHILDREN
DEPARTMENT OF HEALTH

- Programmes addressing mother to child transmission of AIDS;
- Maternal, Child and Woman's Health and Nutrition programme, which received R142 million in 2004/05 and R148 million in 2005/06; [6]
- Distribution of 360 million condoms in 2004/05;
- Full immunisation coverage of 82% of one-year-old infants in the 2003/04 financial year.

DEPARTMENT OF EDUCATION

- The target of enrolling 300 000 grade R learners met in 2004;
- Development of basic infrastructure at schools, including access to water, electricity and sanitation;
- HIV and AIDS and school nutrition – 6.8 million learners received meals during 2004 and R847 million was spent in 2004/05 and R928 million will be spent in 2005/06.

DEPARTMENT OF LABOUR

- Conducts blitz inspections that investigate a number of issues around compliance with legislation, including the BCEA, which makes provision for the fact that children under the age of 15 may not take up employment. Up to March 2004, 187 blitz inspections were conducted;
- The department has requested funding of R4.5 million in 2006/07 for the CLAP with the aim of producing a memorandum for Cabinet outlining the cost implications of this programme. The memorandum will also attempt to identify what government departments have done in terms of child labour and related issues;
- Skills development funding was nearly R52 million in 2004/05 and estimates for 2005/06 are a further R52 million;
- The Umsombomvu Youth Fund has spent R500 million on 90 projects, affecting one million young people with 25 000 jobs created.

DEPARTMENT OF SOCIAL DEVELOPMENT

- The Children, Families and Youth Development programme aims to ensure the empowerment and protection of vulnerable children, youth and families, and has installed a child protection register in seven provinces;
- Children and family benefits received nearly R5 million for the financial year 2005/06;
- The child support grant that currently stands at R180 per month to have an estimated seven million beneficiaries by 2005/06 at a cost of R15 billion;
- A coordinated action plan for orphans and vulnerable children, realising the rights of children affected by HIV, will receive R1.4 million in 2005/06.

THE PRESIDENCY

- The National Youth Commission – to facilitate, coordinate and monitor policies aimed at promoting youth development – will receive nearly R18 million for the financial year 2005/06;
- The ORC, which promotes children's rights by coordinating and monitoring inter-departmental initiatives, to receive R3.5 million for 2005/06.

DEPARTMENT OF SPORT AND RECREATION

- The Lovelife games, receiving R15 million in 2005/06 and R20 million in 2006/07, has a target of 180 185 learners for 2004/05.

DEPARTMENT OF JUSTICE AND CONSTITUTIONAL DEVELOPMENT

- 52 sexual offences courts have been established;
- A play entitled "Speak out", that encourages children to report sexual offences, was presented to 120 359 learners;
- The Child Justice Bill and Sexual Offenders Bill are under development.

DEPARTMENT OF SAFETY AND SECURITY

- Under the programme for detective services, an increase was given over the MTEF period to improve specialised units for child protection and sexual offences, result-ing in 13 099 cases being handled from April to September 2004. R4.8 million and R5 million were allocated for the 2005/06 and 2006/07 financial years respectively.

For the financial year 2004/05 nearly R5 billion was spent on programmes that target children.

ANNEXURE B: SKILLS DEVELOPMENT LEVY FUNDING FLOWS

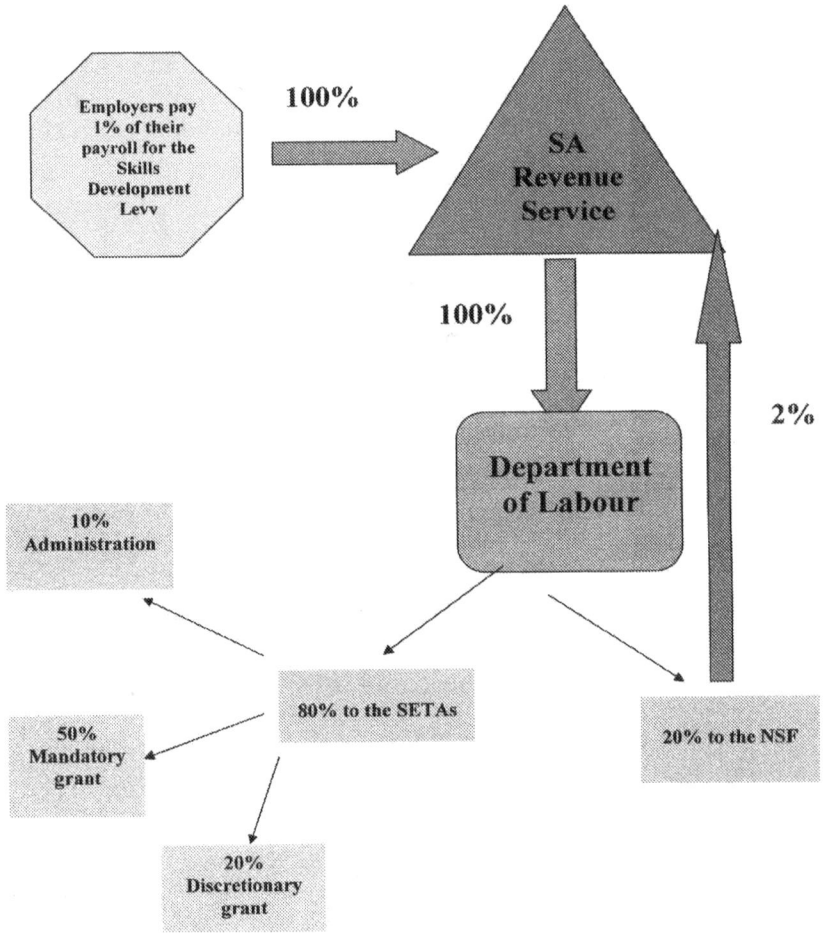

Employers pay 1% of their payroll for the Skills Development Levy

100%

SA Revenue Service

100%

2%

Department of Labour

10% Administration

80% to the SETAs

20% to the NSF

50% Mandatory grant

20% Discretionary grant

REFERENCES

Department of Labour, 2002. *Towards a National Child Labour Action Programme for South Africa: Discussion Document.* In cooperation with the ILO's International Programme on the Elimination of Child Labour (IPEC).

Department of Labour, 2003. *Draft White Paper on the National Child Labour Action Programme for South Africa.* Version 3.1. July. For consideration by government departments and other stakeholders. Unpublished.

Department of Labour, 2005. *Child Labour Action Programme for South Africa (CLAP).* Drafted in cooperation with the ILO's International Programme on the Elimination of Child Labour (IPEC).

Department of Labour, 2005. *National Skills Development Strategy. 1 April 2005 – 31 March 2010.* Pretoria: Department of Labour.

National Treasury, 2005. *Estimates of National Expenditure (ENE) 2005.* Cape Town: Government Printer.

Olarte, A. 2005. *Stories Behind our Stories: Addressing Youth Unemployment.* Accessed at www.pcij.org

Statistics South Africa, 2004. *Labour Force Survey: September 2004.* Pretoria: Statistics South Africa.

Statistics South Africa, 2005. *Labour Force Survey: March 2005.* Pretoria: Statistics South Africa.

United Nations Development Programme South Africa, 2003. *Human Development Report, 2003: The Challenge of Sustainable Development: Unlocking People's Creativity.* Cape Town: Oxford University Press.

---

[1] The ILO defines youth as individuals between the ages of 15 and 24 years.

[2] A study conducted by the Drugs Education and Prevention Research Unit (DEPRU) using time use surveys indicates that work does detrimentally affect school performance.

[3] The Constitution of the Republic of South Africa, Act 108 of 1996.

[4] This is by no means a complete list.

[5] This refers to the South African definition which includes individuals up to the age of 34.

[6] National Treasury Estimates of National Expenditure (ENE), 2005.

CHAPTER 3

IMPLICATIONS OF THE IMPOSSIBILITY OF DEFINING CHILD VULNERABILITY IN A THEORETICALLY RIGOROUS WAY

CHARLES METH[1]

INTRODUCTION

This chapter takes the impossibility of defining vulnerability as its starting point. This fact has disconcerting implications; and this chapter sets itself the task of discovering and confronting them. In short, it poses the question: does the impossibility of defining vulnerability among children in a theoretically rigorous way have implications for the effectiveness of the institutions devised to offer protection against vulnerability? Vulnerability to myriad contingencies is and always has been of the essence of the human condition. As Culpitt says:

> Risk and randomness are the twin "devils" of the chance that is the context of lived life. Hedging against malign peril, gambling on possible windfall luck, and avoiding unreasonable exposure to risk, govern so much of our personal and social experience. Given the obvious fragility of life, and its randomness, individual perception of risk typically provoked reflex responses to private sets of complex fears about health, safety and survival (1999: 3).

Over time, these responses have coalesced into the multifarious arrangements, social and personal (individual or private), characteristic of all societies. Although there are many shared views and values, there are also many culturally specific aspects to what is conceived of as vulnerability and, hence, what it is deemed necessary to protect against. Since vulnerability is a matter of degree (we are all vulnerable) and since the notion of what constitutes vulnerability is at least partly culturally determined, a search for a rigorous concept of vulnerability cannot succeed. Acknowledging this allows us to view the problem from the other end, posing the question: what explains the patterns or institutions of protection against vulnerability observed in particular societies? This, in turn, opens the door to a number of questions to do with the arrangements that have evolved or been created to reduce vulnerability. Prominent amongst these is the question of whether or not the arrangements accord with the society's preferences (always supposing that we can ascertain what these are). From this flows the obvious question of whether or not the arrangements are adequate. Asking the latter question implies that mechanisms for answering it exist, or can be created.

To answer the question of what explains actual patterns of protection against vulnerability, we begin by looking at the notion of social justice, an entry point which directs us straight into the needs- and rights-based approaches to social protection.[2] The limits of the ability of these two approaches to explain the shape of the social protection system are reached quite quickly.

Having exhausted that line of inquiry, we look at the practical notions or concepts of vulnerability used by a variety of actors concerned with the wellbeing of children, in particular the state. The institutions created by the latter, of course, are embodied in legal structures of one sort or another. It is here that the limitations imposed by the normative aspects of vulnerability make themselves most painfully obvious. An attempt is then made, using Marxist political economy, to understand these limitations.

The unlit (partially lit?) corner into which the present chapter dives exists because researchers in the field of child vulnerability and protection, possibly disheartened by the manifest limitations of conventional economics, appear not to have delved too deeply into the economic underpinnings of vulnerability, other than to observe, as most of them do, that poverty lies at the heart of the problem.

Turning for analytical assistance to conventional economics is of little or no avail because the discipline is hamstrung by its blind endorsement of the market (a fault which it seeks to turn to virtue by describing itself as a value-free and objective social science). Economists of leftwing persuasion are not bound by such nonsense. Free of the prejudices of bourgeois economics, they are able to lay the blame for much of the illfare that is found in capitalist economies where it belongs, namely in the absence of the right that few capitalist countries bestow on their citizens, the right to a (decent) job.

Conventional economics (whose role is not to challenge the fundamentals of capitalist economies) is incapable of recognising the significance of the fact that the relationship between individuals and the broader social setting within which they co-exist is constituted (and indeed has to be constituted) in such a manner as to make reproduction of capitalist relations of ownership and production possible. As a result, conventional economics, with its barely concealed contempt for the other social sciences, lacks a plausible set of tools for dealing with the concept of welfare. Insistent though the discipline is on the importance of welfare, it can contribute remarkably little to our understanding of what welfare actually is.

If this chapter has any contribution to make to the debate on child vulnerability, that contribution originates in its insistence on the need for a political economy approach to an understanding of the institutions that are supposed to protect vulnerable children. Before diving into the debate, let us take a brief look at the response of some of the poor to indifferent performance by the state in meeting their justifiable demands.

RIGHTS, SOCIAL UNREST AND SERVICE DELIVERY
South Africa, despite the rights guaranteed the poor by the Constitution, and the oft-asserted centrality of the wellbeing of the poor to policymakers, illustrates the limits of those rights when it comes to delivery, as opposed to rhetoric. A recent, somewhat bleak, analysis by Friedman had this to say on the matter:

> ...many voters do not enjoy the resources that would enable them to organize to be heard in the public policy debate between elections. Their participation is largely limited to expressing their identities in periodic ballots. Because the poor – about two-fifths of the society – are not heard, their experiences and concerns cannot translate into effective policy. This ensures that they remain mired in poverty and excluded, in a continuing vicious cycle, because participation is largely limited to those with the means to organize (Friedman, 2006: 4).

Lacking the capacity for sustained protest on a systematic basis, communities or relatively small groups of individuals within communities respond to continuing deprivation with protests that frequently turn violent. An upsurge of these incidents in recent times suggests that the patience and forbearance shown hitherto by the poor may be giving way to greater activism.[3] This activism, around issues such as lack of housing, sanitation, electricity and water, has seen communities rejecting attempts by political leadership (local and national) to lower social tempers.[4] Children are occasionally at the forefront of such actions. A particularly ghastly incident of this sort occurred in August 2004. A report under the headline "Twenty children shot in Harrismith protest" described how 4 500 children, protesting about service delivery, streamed onto the national highway, leaving the police, according to a spokesperson, with no alternative other than shotgun pellets to disperse them.[5] Incidents of this type are, thankfully, relatively rare – the bulk of the protest action seen in recent years in South Africa appears mainly to involve adults (or at least children do not feature prominently in the reports).

One may view the issues over which adults are most upset as a proxy definition of their sense of vulnerability. It is not possible to elicit a similar definition for children's vulnerability – struggles over children's rights are unlikely to take a similar form. Although it would be heartening if a bottom-up solution to poverty and the problems associated with it in South Africa were to come about, the chances of this happening in the sphere of children's rights in the short- to medium-term are slender. Children may occasionally be drafted into protest movements or action by their parents and/or caregivers, or may even act on their own initiative, but the nature of struggle for the implementation of children's rights is such that it is more likely to be conducted by non-government organisations (NGOs). Children's rights NGOs, well-organised though they undoubtedly are, and speaking with one voice through umbrella bodies, have generally employed a "softly, softly" approach to government. This contrasts strongly with successful single-issue bodies like the Treatment Action Campaign (TAC). Highly militant, the TAC does not hesitate to make use of the courts to challenge the state. Children's rights activists, if they have not already done so, are probably going to have to confront the question of whether or not to adopt a similar approach, at least on problems whose solutions command general agreement, like the poverty at the root of so much vulnerability.[6] The fact that the threats to children's wellbeing are so multifarious, and consequently involve so many different actors, appears, to the outsider, to constitute a significant barrier to joint action. NGO involvement in the securing of children's rights is going to be of as much importance in the future as it has been in the past.

Social justice: Rights, needs and deserts

Children, especially young children, are doubly vulnerable. They rely on adults (or institutions) not only to provide the "reflex responses" to which Culpitt (1999) refers; they depend on adults as well for nurturing, physical and emotional, for the duration of a lengthy childhood. Adults, in turn, have come to rely upon the set of institutions that provide, jointly and severally, what is referred to as social protection against many of the risks faced in day-to-day living. One of the major achievements of mankind, comprehensive social protection, makes social justice, as opposed to the nominal equality before the law that individuals in many countries have long enjoyed, possible. Ensuring that children are protected against as many of the threats to their wellbeing as is possible is thus part of securing social justice. A suitable starting point to begin addressing the question of the nature of the vulnerabilities against which children are to be protected, and of the institutional arrangements for achieving this protection, is thus in the field of social justice.

As one would expect, the notion of social justice is contested. The disagreements over what constitutes social justice play themselves out in the real world as struggles over its definition and over the resources to be allocated to its attainment. It is not necessary for us to dig too deeply into the details of the controversies over social justice here. Suffice it to say that views on social justice of the three major schools of thought in the social sciences, the libertarian (neo-liberal); the utilitarian or liberal/social democratic; and the Marxist, may all be illustrated by reference to their standpoints on rights, needs and deserts, the "...three distinct elements..." of social justice. Following Barr (1998), who, in turn, is summarising the work of Miller (1976), the three elements may be defined as follows:

- "*Rights* – eg political liberty, equality before the law;
- *Deserts* – ie the recognition of each person's actions and qualities;
- *Needs* – ie the prerequisites for fulfilling individual plans of life."

Even if not amenable to "precise theoretical definition...each element is a logically distinct principle embodying a particular type of moral claim". As examples, Barr notes that "deserts" imply that someone who works longer hours should receive more pay; "needs", that someone unable to work should not be left to starve. He then goes on to argue that rights and deserts *can* be reconciled, giving as example the claim that a person should have the right to keep all income legally earned. Less contentious is the proposition that rights and needs *can* be compatible (a sick person should be entitled to healthcare, for example). The real battleground is where deserts and needs meet – the example below is classic:

> ...if I am rich and healthy and you are poor and ill, then either I am taxed (and do not receive my deserts) to pay for your medical treatment, or you receive no treatment (hence your need is not met) so as to protect my deserts (Barr, 1998: 53).

Emphasising, in the text above, the "can" that points to the *possible* reconciliation of rights and deserts and the *possible* compatibility of rights and needs is intended to draw attention to the fact that the nature and extent of the rights, the needs and the deserts in question have an important bearing on whether or not the compatibilities are found and the reconciliations take place. Beyond some basic level, neither rights nor needs may be regarded as absolute in any sense. It is only a slight caricature of politics to say that progressives wish to extend the reach of rights, and the needs that they address, while conservatives seek to limit both. It is also not unduly crude to observe that conservatives generally seek to protect the deserts (the entitlements) of those whose income would furnish the wherewithal for the meeting of needs of those who have not. Arguments advanced in support of such protection vary in strength from Nozick's simple assertion of the right of an individual not to be "robbed" by the state (through) taxation of income legally earned (Barr, 1998: 46) through to the somewhat vaguer fears of the "tyranny of the majority" (the poor, who constitute the majority, voting "...for 'too large' a public expenditure pro-gramme...", a possibility commented on by de Tocqueville in 1835) (Cullis and

Jones, 1992: 110). In addition, the virtue of self-reliance (avoidance of the corrosive power of dependence) is frequently urged upon the poor.

Addressing the problems faced by vulnerable children (a process that involves defining vulnerability in the first instance) entails the discovery of an appropriate balance among rights, needs and deserts. Since socioeconomic life is dynamic, such a balance, if achieved, can never be anything other than dynamic itself.

There is an additional consideration: with varying degrees of enthusiasm, all left-of-centre political movements share the aspirations of liberty, fraternity and equality. The meaning that they attach to each, liberty and equality in particular, may differ, but support for the battle cry is not to be doubted. Of relevance here, is the Marxist perception that:

> Liberty is a much more active concept than the mere absence of coercion. It cannot exist where economic or political power is distributed unequally, nor where the actions of the state are biased...; freedom, moreover, includes a substantial measure of equality and economic security (Barr, 1998: 58).

Widely rejected by conservatives because of its implications (amongst them, demands on the fiscus for the material resources required to make freedom thus conceived a reality),[7] this perception gives notice of what is necessary to make some "rights" a reality. As such, it should stand as a warning to all who prattle about rights without consideration of what is involved in securing them. With this in mind, let us consider, in turn, the needs- and rights-based approaches to social protection to see how much insight they can provide on the question of children's vulnerability.

NEEDS

In an attempt to discover an approximation of the ordering of welfare priorities that could emerge from (an ideal) democratic process we turn to the business of "describing situations in terms of human needs," an approach implicitly frowned upon by human rights advocates. What follows is a trawl though the literature to see if there is any way of specifying, a priori, the needs that must be met if vulnerability is to be minimised. The exploration below is limited in that it concerns itself chiefly with those variables that economists consider, when it is clear that a multidisciplinary approach (looking at both material and emotional needs) is required. The fact that the discussion focuses mainly on economic variables is unfortunate, but not fatal.

The start is not encouraging – conventional economics does not handle the problem of identifying needs very well. Rather it ducks the problem altogether, burying it in pointless discussion about necessities and luxuries and marginal and total utilities, with occasional reference to that historical oddity, the Giffen good. More serious works concerned with welfare, like Nussbaum and Sen's *The Quality of Life* (1993) or Partha Dasgupta's monumental *An Inquiry into Well-Being and Destitution* (2000 [1993]) treat the matter with greater intellectual rigour (and honesty). Dasgupta, for example, states that:

> The claims of needs suggest a sense of urgency. They hint, but only hint, at a preemptory [pre-emptive] argument. Basic needs display these features in a sharp form.

> *We can postpone listening to a piece of music or going to a party, but we can't postpone the consumption of water when thirsty, or food when hungry, or medical attention when ill. Such needs have lexicographic priority over other needs in our own evaluation of goods and services...The meeting of these needs is a prerequisite for the continuation of one's life. Their fulfilment makes life **possible**. For life to be enjoyable, other sorts of goods are required* (2000 [1993]: 39-40, emphasis in original).

This is all very well, but it still leaves us with the problem of distinguishing needs from wants. Theory cannot, however, provide any more guidance than that suggested above. Nevertheless, the distinction must be made in practice, because as Dasgupta argues:

> *Needs provide a most valuable marker for guiding public policy. The observation that needs vary, that there are different types of needs, that there are wants which are not needs, is not much more than a banality. We could make the same observation about wellbeing, or for that matter about preference fulfilment and functionings. But it would be grotesque if these concepts were for that reason banished from the political lexicon. What would political morality then be about?* (2000 [1993]: 40).

At the same time as one acknowledges the force of Dasgupta's argument, one must also admit that approaching the problem of defining vulnerability *a priori* using a needs-based approach does not offer much promise. Although there will be some universals, such as the need for shelter and adequate nutrition, that discovery cannot take us very far. In the absence of a democratic process that reveals preferences,[8] the search for the list of "needs" that must be met if vulnerability is to be held to some acceptable minimum appears to be an inescapably empirical matter. Asserting that developing a definition of vulnerability that enjoys widespread acceptance is an empirical matter cannot eliminate the difficulties inherent in such a process. Children's rights activists are by no means immune to the pleading of special interest groups among their number, seeking to persuade the community in general of the importance of their cause. As Feeny and Boyden (2003: ii)[9] argue:

> *The creation of categories of "especially vulnerable children" such as street children, AIDS orphans and child sex workers has led to disproportionate attention at the expense of other children suffering similar but less visible threats to their protection. It also appears that the vulnerability of such groups is in many cases overstated or misplaced, and being singled out in such a way may unintentionally further their stigmatization.*

From the policy point of view, there can be no halt to the search for vulnerable groups. The needs uncovered in this continual search are likely to change over time. There will also be regionally specific needs. In multi-cultural societies it is also to be expected that there will be differing patterns of needs. A consultative political process is required to rank needs in order of priority if only because, as economists never tire of pointing out, demands are infinite but the resources available to begin satisfying them are not. Individual activist and special interest groups can expend their energies in whatever manner their conscience dictates – at the national level there is no escaping the need for a means of ranking problems in order of severity.

This is no simple task. If democracy really worked (and if children of all ages could articulate their needs), those affected could make known their demands. Means to assess these claims could be developed, and from that could emerge an ordering of the problem, one which would serve as a guide to policymakers and activists alike. From time to time, signals (both of the spontaneous and the systematic sort) do emerge from civil society on aspects of these demands. The information is, however, usually too noisy and the coverage too sketchy to contribute much to sound policy design. Let us see what the rights-based approach has to offer.

RIGHTS[10]

As the leading capitalist economies slowly grew past their brutal periods of primitive accumulation, social protection against contingencies gradually began to supplant private arrangements made to cope with risk. A flurry of activity in the post-World War II period saw the consolidation in many countries of diverse programmes into the comprehensive systems that came to be known as the welfare state. These systems, coupled with steady economic growth, produced states of wellbeing never before experienced among common folk. They performed as well the valuable function of damping down working class resentment at bearing the bulk of the burden of illfare in society. The spirit of the age was captured in the Universal Declaration of Human Rights, adopted in 1948, which sanctioned the growth of rights-based systems. Article 25 of the Declaration states that:

> (1) Everyone has the right to a standard of living adequate for the health and wellbeing of himself and of his family, including food, clothing, housing and medical care and necessary social services, and the right to security in the event of unemployment, sickness, disability, widowhood, old age or other lack of livelihood in circumstances beyond his control.

> (2) Motherhood and childhood are entitled to special care and assistance. All children, whether born in or out of wedlock, shall enjoy the same social protection.

Full compliance with the Declaration is no trivial matter – Article 23 guarantees everyone the right to work (not to a job) and to protection against unemployment. It was not until 1989 that all of the "...standards relating to the specific concerns of children...expressed in legal instruments such as covenants, conventions, and declarations" (www.unicef.org/crc/crc.htm) were brought together in the United Nation's Convention on the Rights of the Child (CRC). These rights are laid out in 41 articles. As one would expect of a document that was ten years in the making, having overcome "[i]nitial indifference and political confrontation" (Pais, 1999: 5), the articles cover almost every eventuality. According to Pais (1999: iv), the significance of a rights-based approach is that it means:

> ...describing situations not in terms of human needs, or areas for development, but in terms of the obligation to respond to the rights of individuals. This empowers people to demand justice as a right, and not as charity.

Although the CRC does not define vulnerability, a definition may be inferred from the rights these instruments confer. In recognising the "right of every child to a standard of living adequate to a child's physical, mental, moral, spiritual and social development," Article 27 of the Convention is implicitly stating that circumstances which deny the child that standard of living (poverty being the most likely), make the child vulnerable to underdevelopment in each of the spheres listed.

Thinking about rights-based protection against vulnerability obliges us to consider the very different forms of intervention required to provide protection. To deal with this problem it is conventional to distinguish between positive and negative rights. The notion derives from a distinction made between those rights which entitle us to make:

> ...a claim **to** something, a share of material goods...or of some particular commodity, such as education when young, and medical attention when in need...A negative right, on the other hand, is a right for something **not** to be done to one, that some particular imposition be withheld. It is a right not to be wronged intentionally in some specified way (Dasgupta, 2000 [1993]: 45, emphasis in original).

Crudely speaking, the ability to guarantee positive rights is a function of the ability of the society to alleviate the worst effects of poverty (or better still, to eradicate it altogether). Negative rights can be guaranteed if a society can:

- Inculcate among adults an intolerance of the flouting of children's rights;
- Create the legal structures and social services necessary to detect and punish wrongdoing when it occurs; and
- Attempt to repair children whose negative rights have been infringed.

This division corresponds (for example) roughly with the division of activities in the national Department of Social Development – on one side there are social grants (now hived off into the South African Social Security Agency) and on the other social services. In practice, infringements of the two types of rights are probably not separated in this tidy fashion – it is almost certainly the case that both are negatively related to income (expenditure) level. The distinction does, however, have its uses – it is probably true to say that in a highly unequal society like South Africa it would be easier to harvest additional taxes required to fund social services when abuse begins to prick the conscience of the well-off. Finding the fiscal resources to tackle poverty by means of social grants for those who fall through the gaps in the social protection system, by contrast, is likely to prove a much harder task. This has implications for the enforcement of positive rights for children.

Although the logic of the rights-based approach to social protection is persuasive, it is not without problems.[11] Recall from the discussion above the assertion that it means:

> ...describing situations not in terms of human needs, or areas for development, but in terms of the obligation to respond to the rights of individuals. This empowers people to demand justice as a right, and not as charity.

The text from which this observation is taken (Pais, 1999) is silent on the question of how the newly empowered are to demand satisfaction of their rights.[12] Not all commentators conflate the existence of a right with the ability to exercise it. In a piece that seeks to put the rights-based approach to development into perspective, Cornwall and Nyamu-Musembi observe that:

> Ultimately, however it is articulated and operationalised by a development agency, a rights-based approach would mean little if it had no potential to achieve a positive transformation of power relations among development actors. It must be interrogated for the extent to which it enables those whose lives are affected most to articulate their priorities and claim genuine accountability from development agencies, and also the extent to which the agencies become critically self-aware and address inherent power inequalities in their interaction with those people (2004: 1432).

A moment's reflection on this statement makes it clear that the nature of the right in question, and that of the "development agency" whose job it is to facilitate its delivery, is critical in determining the likelihood of its being delivered. Within the household, parents or caregivers are, or should be, the guarantors of many negative rights, freedom from abuse of all kinds being one of the more important among them. Transformation of power relations among small children and adults is not achieved by the passage of a bill of rights. Some positive rights are cast in such general terms that it becomes difficult for "development agencies" to act on them. For example, we know that in South Africa millions of poor go hungry. We also know that the Constitution grants everyone the right not to go hungry. Clearly, the existence of the right is not sufficient to prevent hunger. The likely reason for the gap between the promise and the reality is the inability of the poor and/or oppressed to make demands effectively.[13] To put it bluntly, they often lack the political power to enforce their demands.

Cornwall and Nyamu-Musembi (2004: 1417) sum up the different implications for policy implied respectively by "rights-based" and "needs-based" approaches as follows:

> Some commentators...argue that whereas a needs-based approach focuses on securing additional resources for delivery of services to particular groups, a rights-based approach calls for existing resources to be shared more equally and for assisting the marginalised people to assert their rights to those resources. It thus makes the process of development explicitly political. The two can be motivated by radically different things: needs can be met out of charitable intentions, but rights are based on legal obligations (and in some cases ethical obligations that have a strong foundation in human dignity even though they are only in the process of being solidified into legal obligations). Commentators also draw attention to contrasts between the normative force of a rights-based approach and utilitarian-driven approaches such as a "low cost high impact" project approach and cost-benefit analysis. A rights-based approach, for example, is likely to give priority to severe or gross types of rights violations even if these affect only a small number of children, while these other approaches would offer a basis for justifying a focus on less severe types of violations that affect a larger number of children.

One discovers that in practice decisions are made on the basis of both types of approaches. It is not always obvious when this is being done. The death of an infant or child constitutes evidence of the most extreme form of vulnerability and therefore there is a strong case for according the highest priority to policies aimed at reducing child and infant mortality rates. The implications of this suggest:

> ...it is clear that the view that the right to life of infants and under-fives sits squarely within the (normative) rights-based tradition. In so doing it gives "priority to severe or gross types of rights violations even if these affect only a small number of children," and relegates to second place "less severe types of violations that [possibly] affect a larger number of children". Whether the broader society shares this view is something that needs to be ascertained...The political process, which should disclose these preferences, fails for a variety of reasons to do so. That being so, there is no way of knowing if the current budgetary allocations (which constitute an implicit ordering of vulnerabilities) reflect society's choices, the wishes of planners, the predilections of the various ministers of state or the desire of the state to accommodate the multitude of pressure groups seeking to advance particular child rights. Steps to dispel this ignorance are urgently required (Meth, 2005: 27).

What this implies is that there is a need to interrogate actually existing policy the better to understand the imperatives that have given that policy its present shape. Policy to protect children against threats to their wellbeing is informed in South Africa by the Bill of Rights in the Constitution. That document, however, can only offer limited guidance to policymakers. The drafting of law and the creation of institutions to protect children is an immensely complex affair. The interrogation of policy cannot be limited to an examination of the condensation process that translates the threats to children's wellbeing into carefully crafted legal instruments that spell out children's rights. Although these instruments cover almost every contingency against which children require protection, one cannot infer from them any ordering of the severity of the multitudinous threats to children's wellbeing.

Life is breathed into the institutions and practices of child protection by the process of allocating the fiscal and other resources they need to sustain them. Budgetary constraints are real, so too are the limits of the capacity of the various bodies implementing children's rights. Budgetary (and resource) allocations constitute an implicit weighting of the various needs.[14] That weighting corresponds to a definition of vulnerability, ranked in order of the severity of the perceived threat. To reveal the ordering implied by existing allocations, it is necessary to interrogate budgetary processes as well. Discovering whether or not the revealed ordering corresponds with what "society" wants is only possible if that ordering is exposed to the harsh light of day. It is time to debate this matter openly, not flinching in the face of some of the really cruel questions[15] which such a discussion is bound to raise. It is also time to begin raising questions about whether or not the institutions created, legal and other, are appropriate and adequate for the problems they seek to address.

SOCIAL PROTECTION OF CHILDREN IN SOUTH AFRICA

Children may be harmed by acts of commission and of omission. Sexual abuse would be an example of the former. The latter could take two forms, either wilful or involuntary. If a child is prevented from attending school (an important right) because its labour in the fields is necessary the intention would not be to harm the child. Wilfully preventing a child from attending school for cultural reasons would be an act of commission. As such, it is likely to bring the individual or group of individuals responsible into conflict with the authorities, if school attendance is enshrined as a right within the legal system. If a child were to go unfed because the cupboard was bare, that would be an act of involuntary omission. A common unwitting act of omission is that of failing to foster a child's "physical, mental, moral, spiritual and social development" simply for want of the wherewithal or the knowledge of how to do so.

Rights-based approaches attempt to deal with acts of commission and of omission. The "shopping lists" constructed to cover these eventualities yield loose "definitions" of vulnerability. An example of this is to be found in the *White Paper for Social Welfare*. This offers a list of children to be regarded "...as especially vulnerable by policymakers and service delivery agencies" (presumably it was not thought to be exhaustive when written).
It reads as follows:

• Children from birth to 36 months;
• Pre-school children aged three to six years who, because of poverty and/or other factors, have insufficient access to early childhood development services;
• Children requiring out-of-home care;
• Children with disabilities;
• Children with chronic diseases, including HIV/AIDS;
• Children who are abused and neglected;
• Street children;
• Children engaged in labour that decreases their wellbeing;
• Children abusing substances;
• Children of divorcing parents;[16] and
• Children suffering from insufficient nutrition (Cited in Streak and Poggenpoel, 2005: 13).[17]

Finding valid reasons for excluding any of these categories of children from the list would not be easy; if anything we would want to add to the list. Orphanhood, for example, unless it is subsumed under one of the categories, is conspicuous by its absence. Not much imagination is required, however, to see that the problem of identifying those among this list in need or even most in need of welfare services is formidable. The "Save the Children" approach in South Africa, with its focus on orphans and vulnerable children, states that an:

> [O]rphan is a child under 18 who has lost one or both parents; vulnerability will be determined at community level and includes children living with sick parents, children living in poverty, abused, disabled, abandoned, destitute or displaced, including non-national children.[18]

These "definitions" of vulnerability are consistent with the primary instruments seeking to safeguard children's rights: as argued above, the separate elements of the definitions may be derived from the instruments. At an abstract level, the "definitions" of vulnerability reproduced above refer to states or conditions in which unmet needs have arisen or are likely to arise. One set of needs are those that would have been met if positive rights had been honoured, the other if the negative rights had as well.

63

These needs are both material and emotional. Attempts to address both types of needs are made in the constitutional provisions and subsequent legal enactments, to which we now turn.

Social protection in the South African Constitution (1996) is rights-based. The Bill of Rights in the Constitution vouchsafes social security (and sufficient food!) to all, subject to the "available resources" and "progressive realisation" clause (section 27[3]). Children's rights in the Constitution are spelled out in section 28. Fully ten years were to pass before a new piece of legislation, giving effect to the constitutional provisions, was assented to by the President. The Children's Act, Act No 38 of 2005, was passed by the National Assembly plenary in December 2005 and assented to by the President in June 2006 (Government Gazette No 28944). Its passage was not without controversy, stirred up by a provision in the Bill banning the cultural practice of virginity testing (Jamieson and Proudlock, 2006). There is still some way to go before the Act is complete. Provisions omitted from the 2005 Act are contained in an Amendment Bill (tabled in July 2006). After working their way through all of the many stages of the legislative process, these will ultimately be incorporated into a single Act, possibly by 2008 (Jamieson and Proudlock, 2006).

It is worth reproducing in full the objectives of the Children's Act, 2005. Chapter 1, section 2 tells us that they are:

(a) *to promote the preservation and strengthening of families;*
(b) *to give effect to the following constitutional rights of children, namely*
   (i) *family care or parental care or appropriate alternative care when removed from the family environment;*
   (ii) *social services;*
   (iii) *protection from maltreatment, neglect, abuse or degradation; and*
   (iv) *that the best interests of a child are of paramount importance in every matter concerning the child;*
(c) *to give effect to the Republic's obligations concerning the wellbeing of children in terms of international instruments binding on the Republic;*
(d) *to make provision for structures, services and means for promoting and monitoring the sound physical, psychological, intellectual, emotional and social development of children;*
(e) *to strengthen and develop community structures which can assist in providing care and protection for children;*
(f) *to protect children from discrimination, exploitation and any other physical, emotional or moral harm or hazards;*
(g) *to provide care and protection to children who are in need of care and protection;*
(h) *to recognise the special needs that children with disabilities may have; and*
(i) *generally, to promote the protection, development and wellbeing of children.*

Although the (South African) Children's Act (like the United Nations CRC) does not explicitly define vulnerability, it is possible, by working one's way through the objects of the Act, to infer from its provisions a definition of sorts.[19] So, where the preamble of the Children's Act states that every child has the rights set out in the Bill of Rights we can infer, for example, from the provisions in sections 28(1)(c) and (d) granting children the right to basic nutrition, shelter, basic health care services and social services and to be protected from maltreatment, neglect, abuse or degradation, that children may be vulnerable to deprivation of the essentials in (c) and may be subjected to the evils of the above.

It is necessary, however, to be able to more than merely infer definitions of vulnerability from legal instruments, either national or international. To say this is not to suggest that the Children's Act (or the CRC and similar instruments) is not essential, it clearly is. Rather it is to argue that a clearer understanding of the nature and extent of the vulnerability of the nation's children must be sought elsewhere. The reasons why such an understanding is necessary are obvious: guidance is required for those who must frame programmes of action. It is not possible to bid rationally for scarce budgetary resources unless there is some measure of the extent of vulnerability to each of the many threats children face. The search for a concept of vulnerability has thus become a search for a way to express the extent and relative severity of the multitude of threats to children's wellbeing. Although there may be differences of interpretation and emphasis, individual threats are all well enough understood (and defined in the relevant legal documents). It is the combination of threats that needs to be pinned down. This complex question, which we shall not pursue here, appears not to have been addressed systematically.[20]

Instead, we will dive into another murky pool, that containing the question of how the rights enshrined in the Children's Act are to be asserted. There is a tension between the provisions in the Bill of Rights as they apply to children and the Children's Act of 2005 which is supposed (intended) to give effect to them. Before considering it, let us look briefly at the response of (some of) the poor in South Africa to the perceived failure of the state to live up to the promise of the Constitution.

RIGHTS ENFORCEMENT: TENSION BETWEEN THE ACT AND THE CONSTITUTION

At the beginning of this chapter it was asserted that the involvement of NGOs in securing children's rights was unlikely to diminish in intensity in the future. The reasons we are likely to see an increase in NGO activity (rather than the reduction one might have looked forward to after the monumental task of participating in the creation of the Children's Act of 2005 had been completed) become clearer when we look at the problems of enforcement.

The Children's Act of 2005, product of a long consultation process closely involving most of the organisations concerned with children's rights (Proudlock, 2005), gives effect to constitutional rights by specifying those rights, as we have seen above, in some detail and by laying down a set of penalties for contraventions of the various provisions of the laws protecting children (according them negative and positive rights).

Enforcement of the Act is discussed in chapter 20, section 5 which spells out the offences it envisages. Section 305(3)(a) and (b) and section 305(4) for example identify a series of offences, all of which take the form of a failure to meet the provisions of the Bill of Rights. Responsibility for discharging the duties in question (they secure children's rights not to be abused, deliberately neglected,[21] to have adequate food, clothing, lodging and medical assistance), rests upon a responsible individual or individuals (parents, guardians, caregivers and the like). In this, the Act follows Article 27 of the UN's CRC and Article 20(1) of the African Charter on the Rights and Welfare of the Child (ACRWC) (Rosa and Dutschke, 2006: 14).

Relief can presumably only be granted by the courts on a case-by-case basis. Under conditions of mass poverty, large number of people may, through no fault of their own, deprive children of adequate food, shelter, clothing and medical attention. If the children concerned are to assert their rights, there would be little point in bringing an action against responsible individuals whose poverty prevents them from discharging the duties the law requires of them. Rather, one imagines, the route to relief would lie through section 27(1)(c) of the Constitution, which guarantees right of access to "social security, including if they are unable to support themselves and their dependants, appropriate social assistance". Therefore insofar as contraventions of the Children's Act occur because the responsible individuals (those with the legal liability to make the relevant provision) are too poor to comply, the Act cannot give effect to the relevant provisions of the Constitution.

Even though the Children's Act is at present not yet in force, this matter has already begun to exercise the minds of those who have struggled (and continue to struggle) hard and long for children's rights. Rosa and Dutschke (2006) have addressed the problem, noting that "there is still uncertainty as to:

- How children's rights should be interpreted;
- What the content of each right is;
- What the extent and nature of the obligations placed on the government are; and
- How this can be translated into practical delivery" (2006: iii).

Since the Children's Act is not yet in force it is necessary to search for clues in the jurisprudence of the Constitutional Court. The signs are not encouraging. Rosa and Dutschke include details of the well-known *Grootboom* case and an analysis of the Constitutional Court judgment in their paper (2006: 19). This case offers one of the few indications of how the courts view the respective responsibilities of parents and the state. In essence, the Constitutional Court's position seems to be that the state is not obliged to meet the section 28(c) rights (in the *Grootboom* case the right to shelter) on demand. The order requiring the state to provide shelter was made in terms of section 26, which deals with people's rights to adequate housing. It was found that the state had not taken reasonable steps to ensure that its housing policies could meet the needs of people in crisis (Rosa and Dutschke, 2006: 19-20). We see the rights-based approach in action when it comes to defining what the "reasonableness" standard is that is used to assess a state programme, in the *Grootboom* case its housing programme. Rosa and Dutschke list six conditions:

- *"The programme must be reasonable in conception and implementation;*
- *It must be balanced and flexible;*
- *It must pay attention to crisis situations;*
- *It must deal with long-, medium- and short-term needs;*

- *It may not exclude a significant segment of society; and finally*
- *The programme must prioritise the needs of the most desperate"* (2006: 20).

Unlike the section 27(1) rights, which are qualified in section 27(2) by the "weasel" clause which requires the state to take "reasonable legislative and other measures" to "achieve the progressive realisation" of the rights "within its available resources," the section 28 rights are "not qualified by reference to reasonable measures, progressive realization or resource constraints" (Rosa and Dutschke, 2006: 15-16). If the primary agents (the parents, for example) responsible for ensuring that a child's section 28 rights are met fail to do so by virtue of their poverty, then presumably if they were prosecuted they would be able to claim that in their case the state had not taken reasonable steps to ensure that children living with their families could enjoy the section 28 rights.[22] They could also appeal through the Court for "appropriate social assistance" referred to in section 27(1)(c). The Court would then have to assess the reasonableness of the state's programmes for meeting the section 28 requirements, and, if these were found wanting and further relief in the form of social assistance was denied, it would also have to assess the reasonableness of the social assistance provided in terms of section 27(1)(c).

Poor parents or caregivers of poor children are unlikely to be able to pursue these sources of relief without assistance. The likelihood is that when the test cases take place, they will do so with the backing of one of the NGOs who take it upon themselves to handle such matters. When the Expanded Public Works Programme (EPWP) is operating at full steam, and there is sufficiently high take-up of the Child Support Grant, the state's defence will almost certainly be that a reasonable programme of social assistance has been created. Except where the state is shown to have failed in its duty to "pay attention to crisis situations" or to "prioritise the needs of the most desperate," applicants to the Court for relief are going to have to show that the government programme in question is not reasonable, which could be a difficult task.

There is another route, namely through the concept of "minimum core obligations". The progressive realisation clause was referred to, possibly unfairly, as a weasel clause because of the ease with which the state could hide insufficient progress towards realisation of the rights contemplated in sections 27(1)(a), (b) and (c) of the Constitution behind the "available resources" qualification. The minimum core obligations condition closes this escape route.[23] Like the CRC, this provision has its origins in another international covenant, the International Covenant on Economic, Social and Cultural Rights (ICESCR). It offers, through General Comments issued by its supervisory body, the Committee on Economic, Social and Cultural Rights (CESCR), interpretations of the rights embodied in the Covenant. Discussing the minimum core, Rosa and Dutschke note that:

> The CESCR has stated that apart from the duty to realise a socioeconomic right progressively, "a minimum core obligation to ensure the satisfaction of, at the very least, **minimum essential levels of each of the rights** is incumbent on every State party". The standard of a minimum core can be translated to mean that a minimum level of subsistence is necessary for a dignified human existence. What the minimum core

*consists of must be read from the ICESCR and the General Comments made in rela-
tion to the individual rights. The CESCR has delineated these minimum levels in relation to the right to adequate housing, the right to adequate food, the right to education, the right to the highest attainable standard of health and the right to water. The
concept of a minimum core applies to both adults' and children's socioeconomic
rights* (2006: 12-13 [emphasis in original]).

Both the Constitution and the Children's Act require the state to conform to the
requirements of international instruments "binding" on it. South Africa has ratified
the UN's CRC, but has only signed the ICESCR. This means that the provisions of
the latter are not binding, which means in turn that South Africa's obligations are
limited to not taking steps "which defeat the object and purpose of the treaty" (Rosa
and Dutschke, 2006: 17). These authors are of the opinion, however, that in the light
of South Africa's commitment to international law "that everyone should have the
right to a minimum core of basic entitlements" (2006: 26). An attempt was made to
use the minimum core argument in the *Grootboom* case for the right of access to
adequate housing. It was rejected by the Court on the grounds that, "...there are
practical difficulties with ascertaining the varying degree of needs in the country
and that there is a lack of information on what these needs are" (2006: 27). The
wheel has thus come full circle – rights cannot be addressed because needs cannot
be determined.

Rosa and Dutschke (2006) begin their paper with an analysis of poverty among
children. Yet a distressing feature of the precedents established by the Court thus far,
in falling back on the provision that locates primary responsibility for meeting
children's rights on the parents, is an apparent underplaying of:

> *...the fact that many parents are willing but financially unable to provide the stan-
> dard of living that children have a right to in terms of the CRC and the AfCRWC*
> (Rosa and Dutschke, 2006: 23).

If children rights are to be honoured, the poverty of the households in which they
live requires greater acknowledgement than the provision of Child Support Grants
and the remainder of the "social wage". In the absence of the right to decent paid
employment, which no capitalist society offers, social assistance for adults, which
many do offer, is the only reasonable alternative.

WHAT OF THE FUTURE?

South Africa is committed to the modest goals of halving poverty and unemployment (poverty's major cause) by 2014. So large are the numbers of poor and unemployed that even if these goals are attained (which is unlikely) a very large number
of people in both predicaments will remain (Meth, 2006a). Adult and child alike will
see at least some of their rights going unfulfilled (their needs unmet), unless the
state can be persuaded, through the Court, that the existing social protection system
is inadequate, ie that the state has not taken reasonable steps to ensure that rights
are progressively realised.

It is clear that for children's rights to be met a minimum condition (necessary but
not sufficient) is that their caregivers be raised out of the poverty which prevents
millions of them from discharging their responsibilities. One of the problems to be

faced in confronting the state over the "reasonableness" of its programmes for addressing the needs of the poor is the fact that no blueprint for a comprehensive social protection system exists. Much energy and resources are going into the provision of the social wage (health, education, housing, electricity, water, sanitation and social grants for certain categories of beneficiary), but little attention is paid to income poverty, from whose importance government seeks to distract attention by repeated references to the advances it has made in the provision of the social wage (Meth, 2006b). Of late, extravagant claims about the success in reducing income poverty have been added to the state's armoury of weapons to deploy against critics (Meth, 2006c; 2006d).

With the exception of the extension of the Child Support Grant, the recommendations of the Taylor Committee of Inquiry (2002) on comprehensive social assistance, in particular the call for a Basic Income Grant, have largely been ignored. Repeated references to a comprehensive social protection system are made by senior politicians but the social assistance component of the system is never given any content. Slighting references to social assistance as the dole and claims that "our people want the dignity of work, not handouts" (true, but not relevant in the face of the manifest inability of the economy to provide jobs for all who need them) seem to be part of a softening-up campaign to prepare people for a stripped-down safety net-type approach to social protection for adults. The strong likelihood is that we will see government offer the EPWP, enlarged somewhat from its present size, as an alternative to social assistance for the working age population. It is in the nature of such programmes that the wage must be set so low that it will not entice informal economy workers, domestic workers and all of the other poorly paid workers out of their existing employment. In other words, the principle of less eligibility, enunciated by the Royal Commission set up to look at the Poor Law in Britain in 1832, with all the horrors their recommendations entailed (Barr, 1998: 16-17) must apply. Those who refuse such work (as a substitute for social assistance) will probably be deemed to have defined themselves to be not poor. Those who accept it, and there will be many who do so with gratitude, will still be poor, but less than they are today.

The struggle for children's rights is inextricably bound up with the broader struggle for rights for all and in particular the fight against poverty and unemployment (and the AIDS epidemic that exacerbates both). Until such time as the income security of the poor can be guaranteed, children's rights stand in danger of being trampled on.

Services long since identified as being urgently required have to be delivered to the children needing them. These are to be provided in a manner consistent with government's goal of making social services "developmental". Government is aware that to do so an "holistic integrated policy framework" is necessary (Streak and Poggenpoel, 2005: 16). There is, however, much that has to be done before the necessary structures come into being. Problems recognised long ago by the state as requiring an approach that integrates the activities of several departments (joined-up or holistic solutions in jargon-speak) fester on for want of integration. In part this is because it is impossible to define vulnerability rigorously and to rank the threats to children's wellbeing in a consistent manner.[24] As a consequence, the various forms that vulnerability take appear, to an outsider like myself, to be addressed in an ad hoc fashion.

A starting point for an analysis of how well or otherwise government is doing in its attempts to help meet children's needs is with the budgets of the various spheres of government. So, apart from the need to fight for truly comprehensive social protection, there is also a strong imperative to render the process by which funds are allocated to the various aspects of child protection more transparent. In his address to the National Assembly on the tabling of the 2006 Medium Term Budget Policy statement on 25 October 2006, the Minister of Finance announced, no doubt proudly, and not unreasonably so, that South Africa has been ranked fourth out of 59 countries for the transparency of the budget documents by a coalition of international NGOs under the umbrella of the International Budget Project.

One would not wish to take any of the shine off this achievement, but as the Minister admitted himself, "there is still too little debate in this House and in the country on budget priorities". If regard is had for the parlous state of affairs as far as budgeting for children is concerned, then the performance of some of the 55 countries behind South Africa in the ranking referred to above must be pretty dire. A sober analysis of the budget process in South Africa as it affects children (which casts little light on how actual allocations are derived) was unable to answer a number of vital questions on expenditure to meet children's rights (Streak and Poggenpoel, 2005). According to these authors it proved to be impossible to "...identify child-specific spending on social welfare services" or "to shed any light on the size of the funding gap that exists in government's budgeting for social welfare services" (2005: 42).

To understand children's wellbeing, it is necessary to go beyond what is spent directly on them to the indirect expenditures that go to improve their lives. In short, if policy towards children is to be evidence-based rather than instinctual there is a great deal of work to be done.

REFERENCES

Barr, Nicholas. 1998. *The Economics of the Welfare State* (3rd Edition), Oxford: Oxford University Press.

Bhorat, Haroon & Kanbur, Ravi (eds). 2006. *Poverty and Policy in Post-Apartheid South Africa*, Cape Town: HSRC.

Byrne, David. 2000. *Social Exclusion*, Buckingham: Open University Press.

Coetzee, Erika & Streak, Judith. 2004. *Monitoring Child Socio-Economic Rights in South Africa: Achievements and Challenges*, Cape Town: IDASA.

Cole, Ken; Cameron, John & Edwards, Chris. 1983 [1991]. *Why Economists Disagree: The Political Economy of Economics*, London: Longman.

Cornwall, A. & Nyamu-Musembi, C. 2004. "Putting the rights-based approach to development into perspective," *Third World Quarterly*, 25(8).

Cullis, John & Jones, Philip. 1992. *Public Choice and Public Finance: Analytical Perspectives*, London: McGraw-Hill.

Culpitt, Ian. 1999. *Social Policy & Risk*, London: Sage Publications.

Dasgupta, Partha. 1993 [2000]. *An Inquiry into Well-being and Destitution*, Oxford: Clarendon Press.

Dean, Hartley. 2001. "Poverty and Citizenship: Moral Repertoires and Welfare Regimes", in Wilson *et al*, (eds).

Department of Social Development. 2002. *Transforming the Present – Protecting the Future: Report of the Committee of Inquiry into a Comprehensive System of Social Security for South Africa,* (Consolidated Report) referred to as the Taylor Report), Pretoria.

Feeny, Thomas & Boyden, Jo. 2003. *Children and Poverty. A Review of Contemporary Thought on Children and Poverty: Rethinking the Causes, Experiences and Effects,* (Part 1), Christian Children's Fund.

Friedman, Steven. 2006. "A Voice for Some: South Africa's Ten Years of Democracy," in Piombo and Nijzink (eds).

Jamieson, Lucy & Proudlock, Paula (ed). 2006. *Children's Bill Progress Update,* Children's Institute, University of Cape Town, March.

Lal, Deepak & Myint, H. 1996. *The Political Economy of Poverty, Equity and Growth: A Comparative Study,* Oxford: Clarendon Press.

Lawson, Tony. 2003. *Reorienting Economics,* London: Routledge.

Liebenberg, Sandra & Pillay, Karrisha (eds). 2000. *Socio-Economic Rights in South Africa: A Resource Book,* The Socio-Economic Rights Project, University of the Western Cape, October.

Meth, Charles. 2005. "Reflections on the Difficulties of Identifying and Protecting Vulnerable Children and Orphans," unpublished paper prepared for Save the Children UK, School of Development Studies, University of KwaZulu-Natal. June.

Meth, Charles. 2006a. "Half Measures Revisited: The ANC's Unemployment and Poverty Reduction Goals," in Bhorat and Kanbur (eds).

Meth, Charles. 2006b. "Sticking to the Facts: Official and Unofficial Stories about Poverty and Unemployment in South Africa," paper presented at the DPRU/TIPS Conference, Johannesburg.

Meth, Charles. 2006c. "What was the Poverty Headcount in 2004 and How Does it Compare with Recent Estimates by van der Berg *et al?*", SALDRU Working Paper, Southern African Labour and Development Research Unit, University of Cape Town, June.

Meth, Charles. 2006d. "Income Poverty in 2004: A Second Encounter with the Recent van der Berg *et al* Figures", Working Paper, School of Development Studies, University of KwaZulu-Natal, September.

Miller, David. 1976. *Social Justice,* Oxford: Oxford University Press. (Cited in Barr, 1998).

Nussbaum, Martha C. & Sen, Amartya (eds). 1995 [1993]. *The Quality of Life,* Oxford: Clarendon Press.

Pais, Marta Santos. 1999. *A Human Rights Conceptual Framework for UNICEF,* Florence, Italy: UNICEF.

Piombo, Jessica & Nijzink, Lia (eds). 2006. *Electoral Politics in South Africa: Assessing the First Democratic Decade,* Cape Town: HSRC Press.

Proudlock, Paula. 2005. "Children's Bill Update," briefing document, Children's Institute, University of Cape Town, 23 April. Available at www.pmg.org.za, accessed 17 May 2005.

Rosa, S & Dutschke, M. 2006. "Child Rights at the Core: A Commentary on the Use of International Law in South African Court Cases on Children's Socio-Economic Rights," A Project 28 Working Paper, Cape Town: Children's Institute, University of Cape Town.

Republic of South Africa. 1997. *Government Gazette,* Vol. 386, No. 18166, Pretoria, 8 August. Notice 1108 of 1997. Ministry for Welfare and Population Development. *White Paper for Social Welfare.*

Streak, Judith & Poggenpoel, Sasha. 2005. "Towards Social Welfare Services for All Vulnerable Children in South Africa: A Review of Policy Development, Budgeting and Service Delivery," IDASA Occasional Paper, Children's Budget Unit, Budget Information Service.

Wilson, Francis; Kanji, Nazneen & Braathen, Einar (eds). 2001. *Poverty Reduction: What Role for the State in Today's Globalized Economy?* London and New York: Zed Books; Cape Town: New Africa Education Publishing.

---

[1] As I did in the longer work from which this paper is drawn (Meth, 2005), I wish to express heartfelt gratitude to Rachel Bray, Selwyn Jehoma, Annie Leatt, Pat Naicker, Fiona Napier, Michael Noble, Laura Poswell, David Woods, Ingrid Woolard and Gemma Wright (in alphabetical order) and especially to my partner Anna McCord. Naturally any errors in the original and in the present paper are my responsibility.

[2] For want of a better term the whole apparatus intended to guard children against the manifold threats to their wellbeing will be referred to henceforth as social protection. Although the threats they face differ, a similar set of mechanisms and institutions is required to protect adults as well.

[3] A list of protest actions, drawn from just one newspaper, the *Mail & Guardian*, gives a flavour of the mood among sections of the poor. Service delivery failures feature prominently among the causes of the disturbances. "March draws attention to plight of homeless", Hila Bouzaglou, 20 September 2006. "Khutsong: 'The ANC sold us' ", 22 February 2006. The report says that: "The cause of unrest is economic. People are fed up waiting for jobs and basic services such as electricity, clean water and sanitation." "Eleven arrested in North West service protest", 23 January 2006. "Three injured in southern Cape service protest", 16 January 2006. In this instance: "police threw stun grenades and fired rubber bullets at protesting Power Town informal settlement residents". "A winter of discontent", Marianne Merten, 27 May 2005. This article contains a catalogue of the incidents in the first five months of the year. Although the list of incidents in the Merten article is long, President Mbeki was still able to argue, and not implausibly, that as yet, "urban unrest over service delivery" has not yet reached the point that would suggest that the country is threatened by the "centrifugal tensions" that have caused collapse elsewhere in Africa. He claimed further that neither these demonstrations nor minority mobilisation present "any immediate danger to our democracy", "Urban unrest could lead to conflict, says Mbeki", *Mail & Guardian*, 25 May 2005, online version.

Growing community assertiveness is not entirely unexpected. Writing a few years ago, Good (2001, p.47) pointed out "the extent of the demobilization in South Africa should not be exaggerated" in spite of the "...systematic (and astonishingly rapid) process of political demobilization..." that took place after 1994 which left many of the institutions of civil society that represent the poor in a weak state. Some commentators, Desai (2002), for example, and Raj Patel and Richard Pithouse, as an article in *Mail & Guardian* May 20 to 26, 2005 attests, are quite upbeat about the potential of groups representing the interests of the poor.

[4] It remains to be seen whether steps taken by the likes of the Housing Minister to address the frustrations of the unhoused and poorly-housed can succeed before "other festering problems adding to the explosive mix" result in major confrontations. The article from which these comments are drawn, by Linda Ensor, appeared under the headline "Protests signal that the patience of SA's poor is wearing thin" in *Business Day*, 31 May 2005, online version.

[5] See *Mail & Guardian*, 30 August 2004, online edition.

[6] Campaigns around poverty reduction are difficult to mount and sustain. The Basic Income Grant (BIG) coalition is probably the closest thing that there is to an organisation with a focus of this sort – but it has either been ignored or brushed aside by government.

[7] The long passage below from the pens of two prominent libertarians, Lal and Myint (1996), laced with contempt (and alarm), shows that conservatives are under no illusion about the implications of demands for "rights" to be met. They state that:

"The locus and nature of the argument of those who want to use the state to promote egalitarianism has...shifted in a subtle way. In the past such activists, who sought to transform society through state action, usually argued in favour of some form of revolution whereby the anointed would seize power and irreversibly transform society, if necessary by indoctrination to create a New Man. With the revolutionary route at least tarnished by the hideous outcomes in Communist countries – which even fellow-travellers now concede – a new constitutional mania has set in. This emphasizes substantive social and economic rights in addition to the well-known rights to liberty – freedom of speech, contract, and association amongst the most important – emphasized by classic liberals. It seeks to use the law to enforce these rights, based partly on needs, and partly on the 'equality of respect' desired by a heterogeneity of self-selected minorities differentiated by ethnicity, gender and/or sexual orientation. But no less than in the collectivist societies that have failed, this attempt to define and legislate a newly discovered and dense structure of rights (including for some activists those of non-human plants [sic] and animals) requires a vast expansion of government's power over people's lives. Their implementation moreover requires – at the least – some doctoring of the market mechanism" (Lal and Myint, 1996: 314-315).

8 The market, tried and trusted revealer of less fraught preferences, is of even less use than any of the processes discussed here.

9 The paper by Feeny and Boyden (2003) was brought to my attention by Ms Annie Leatt of the Children's Institute in Cape Town. It came a bit late in the day for all the critical insights it offers to be incorporated into the present paper. It is unlikely that I have not fallen into some the numerous traps for unwary travellers in the land of the vulnerable to which it draws attention.

10 Conservatives are scornful of the rights approach, dismissing it as "'rights chatter' – the clamour for numerous and newly discovered individual rights..." They see the granting of rights as part of the explanation of the crisis of the welfare state, and observe that "It is then particularly ironical that, at a time when the welfare state is coming to be repudiated by its progenitors, international institutions such as UNDP, UNICEF, and WIDER are seeking their extension in the Third World" (Lal and Myint, 1996: 381).

11 As Cornwall and Nyamu-Musembi (2004: 1419) observe "Rights-talk can function differently from different mouths. It depends who is speaking about rights and where they are speaking...The same language that may be rhetorical fluff in one place may be words of extreme courage and radical change in another. The use of rights-talk in Washington or Paris might be used piously as new words for the same old liturgy in the cathedrals of international trade and development...But from another place (a slum or the scene of a rigged election) and spoken from another voice (that of poor man or a woman rights lawyer) the same words of rights-talk could function prophetically as a redress to change and challenge power."

12 One of the empowerment tools is the accessible and highly informative resource book on socioeconomic rights edited by Liebenberg and Pillay (2000). It would be interesting to know what use had been made of it. The publication is being updated and an electronic version is being developed. pers comm. Sibonile Khoza, University of the Western Cape, May 2005.

13 The landmark *Grootboom* case that "...gave rise to South Africa's watershed Constitutional Court ruling on socioeconomic rights" has not been followed by a decision "...about government's fulfilment of its obligations based on the unqualified socioeconomic rights given to children..." (Coetzee and Streak, 2004: 61 and 63).

14 It has the feel (to an outsider) of an attempt to do everything. The impression created by the literature is that this leads to most things being done badly.

15 As an example medical doctors, labouring under constraints of time and shortages of supplies of vital drugs and equipment, are compelled to make uncomfortable decisions about where (on which patient) to concentrate their scarce resources.

16 It is important to note that the way in which some of the conditions are specified is crude. Not all 0-3 year olds, for example, are vulnerable in the sense in which the term is generally used – the vulnerability of those with the good fortune to be born into comfortable circumstances and with caring parents is the possibility of the loss of those circumstances. Similarly, in a small but probably not insignificant number of cases, being the children of divorcing parents may mark an improvement in a child's welfare.

17 Some of the details of what these conditions imply are examined in Robinson and Biersteker (1997, pp.66-67).

18 *pers comm.* Ms Fiona Napier, Save the Children (UK), Pretoria, May 2005.

19 It is also possible to infer a definition of vulnerability from the definition of "care" in section 1 of the Act.

20 In Meth (2005) I sketched a direction in which such an inquiry might have to travel and began asking some of the harsh questions that entailed.

21 One wonders why the term "deliberate neglect" is used so explicitly? It occurs again in section 46(1)(h)(v), which allows a Children's Court to make an order allowing a hospital to retain a child where there are reasonable grounds for believing it has been subjected to "deliberate neglect". Is this an acknowledgement of the likelihood of unintentional neglect occurring mainly as a result of the incapacity of the responsible person to discharge their duties? The definition of neglect: "a failure in the exercise of parental responsibilities to provide for the child's basic physical, intellectual, emotional or social needs" (section (1)) does not help very much.

22 Rosa and Dutschke (2006: 19-20) point out: "The State's obligations towards children who live in the family environment were to provide the legal and administrative infrastructure necessary to ensure that children are afforded the protection encapsulated in section 28. This should be done by providing families with access to adequate housing and other socioeconomic rights on a programmatic and coordinated basis."

23 The progressive realisation clause, Rosa and Dutschke (2006: 10) remind us, was not intended to be used as an escape clause, rather it "...reflects a realistic acceptance that lack of resources – financial and other resources – can hamper the full implementation of economic, social and cultural rights in some States..."

24 The rudiments of a ranking structure are visible in the pyramid depicting four levels of social services; continuum of care; statutory services; early intervention; and prevention, and the stress is laid on the need to shift away from a concentration of resources in care towards prevention. This does not, however, identify specific threats to children's wellbeing (Streak and Poggenpoel, 2005: 17).

CHAPTER 4

CHILD LABOUR AND HIV/AIDS IN SOUTH AFRICA:
A HUMAN RIGHTS PERSPECTIVE

CHRISTELE DIWOUTA TIKI

INTRODUCTION

The United Nations (UN) Convention on the Rights of the Child (CRC) indicates a shared and increasing support and acknowledgment by the world of the importance of protecting and promoting children's rights. However, the advent of HIV/AIDS introduces a new threat to the realisation and enjoyment of these rights in many developing nations.

This chapter analyses the relationship between child labour and HIV/AIDS in South Africa, through the prism of international, regional and national standards relating to children's rights. It also highlights the crisis of orphaning occasioned by AIDS which has led to an increase in the phenomenon of child-headed households.

The CRC and other human rights instruments relating to children's rights are under-pinned by four principles: non-discrimination; participation; survival and develop-ment; and the best interests of the child. Each of these is greatly threatened by the pandemic. In this regard, this chapter considers the implementation of the human rights instruments ratified by South Africa as well as assesses the approach to child labour in relation to HIV/AIDS.

In 1994, the first democratically elected government came to power. South Africa, which had been known for its brutal and segregationist rule, was now a free and democratic state but with major challenges of reconciliation, economic justice and development to consider. After the transition, and despite the challenges, South Africa had to meet its international obligations. The new democratic state rapidly complied by signing and ratifying most existing international legal instruments, including those directed at protecting the rights of the child.

INTERNATIONAL STANDARDS

THE UNITED NATIONS CONVENTION ON THE RIGHTS OF THE CHILD

Numerous human rights instruments have been adopted under the auspices of the UN – many were of relevance to children, as human rights generally include those of children (Viljoen, 2003: 215) – but before the CRC[1] none dealt explicitly with the rights of children. The CRC has been widely signed and ratified by states the world over with the exception of the United States and Somalia.[2]

South Africa ratified the CRC in 1997, meaning that it is compelled to take action to bring its law, policy and practice into line with the relevant international provsions. According to Articles 43 and 44, South Africa as a ratifying state undertakes to report on the progress made in implementing the CRC to the UN Committee on the Rights of the Child.

At the time the CRC was drawn up, HIV/AIDS was not perhaps considered a major threat to humankind; hence, the CRC does not specifically mention the pandemic. However, the preamble stresses that there are children living in "exceptionally diffi-cult circumstances and that such children need special consideration". This provision seems to be far-reaching and all-encompassing when it comes to child labour and HIV/AIDS.

The CRC is the main international instrument pertaining to children's rights. It is broad in content and covers a wide range of rights. However, most of these rights are not analysed in depth. For instance, the issue of child labour is not stated in the Convention. There is no clear-cut definition of "child labour" but it is taken to mean employment of children under the age of physical maturity in jobs requiring long hours.[3] To some, child labour will also include child prostitution and child soldiering.[4] For practical purposes, child labour needs to be clarified to avoid confusion. It has been posited that not all child labour is necessarily harmful. As pointed out:

> *Children's work needs to be seen as happening along a continuum, with destructive or exploitative work at one end and beneficial work – promoting or enhancing children's development without interfering with their schooling, recreation and rest – at the other. And between these two poles are vast areas of work that need not negatively affect a child's development.[5]*

For the purpose of this discussion, child labour is seen as any activity that prevents a child from fully enjoying the privileges and rights attached to childhood as enshrined in national and international legal instruments. While the issue of child labour is not stated in the Convention, there are a number of instruments that the UN has instituted which address these concerns: the International Labour Organisation (ILO) Minimum Age Convention and the ILO Worst Forms of Child Labour Convention are discussed below.

The ILO Minimum Age Convention, 1973

This Convention provides that children should not engage in economic work before they are 15 years old. They can however engage in light work which is unlikely to be harmful to their health, development or schooling when they are between 12 and 15.[6]

The ILO Worst Forms of Child Labour Convention, 1999

This Convention requires ratifying governments to take measures to immediately abolish the "worst forms of child labour", which include slavery, child prostitution, using a child for illegal activities, and work which by its nature or the circumstances is likely to harm the health, safety or morals of children.[7] South Africa ratified this ILO Convention on 7 June 2000.

REGIONAL STANDARDS

The African Charter on the Rights and Welfare of the Child

The African Charter on the Rights and Welfare of the Child (ACRWC),[8] adopted by the Assembly of the African Union,[9] is based on the African Charter on Human and Peoples' Rights'[10] principle of the supremacy of human rights.[11] Article 3 of the ACRWC further proclaims that every child is entitled to all the rights and freedoms recognised and guaranteed therein, without distinction of any kind.

The ACRWC is further based on the Declaration on the Rights and Welfare of the African Child, 1979,[12] which recognises the need to take appropriate measures to promote and protect the rights and welfare of the African child. The rationale for an African Charter is that the instrument is seen to be more reflective of African cultural norms and concerns. For instance, the ACRWC touches on issues such as the position of the girl child in society, the collectiveness of rights and community responsibilities, the use of children in armed conflicts and refugee children.

THE SOUTH AFRICAN CONSTITUTION

South Africa has domesticated these international and regional instruments, reflecting the country's commitment to global human rights standards and principles. The Bill of Rights in the South African Constitution applies to all people, including children. Section 7(1) states that the Bill of Rights is the "cornerstone of democracy in South Africa". It enshrines the rights of all people in South Africa and affirms the "democratic values of human dignity, equality and freedom."[13] Furthermore, the Constitution recognises that children and youth are a vulnerable group that needs special protection and promotion of their rights. Section 28 sets out a range of rights that apply to all people under the age of 18.

Section 28 of the Bill of Rights gives expression to the principles enshrined in the Convention and establishes the constitutional principle that "a child's best interests are of paramount importance in every matter concerning the child". Every child has the right to, among other things, basic nutrition, protection from maltreatment and neglect, and protection from exploitative labour practices.

THE PROMOTION OF EQUALITY AND THE PREVENTION OF UNFAIR DISCRIMINATION ACT 4 OF 2000

Referred to as "the mother of all equality legislation in South Africa"(Shadrack, 2001: 123), the equality clause in the Constitution obliges the state to enact national legislation "to prevent or prohibit unfair discrimination". The Promotion of Equality and the Prevention of Unfair Discrimination Act, known as the Equality Act, is an example of legislation enacted by the state to take further steps to promote equality and to eradicate unfair discrimination through legal means. Discrimination has been defined by the Act as:

Any act or omission, including a policy, law, rule, practice, condition or situation, which directly or indirectly
  a) Imposes burdens, obligations or disadvantage on;
  b) Withholds benefits, opportunities and advantages from, any person on one or more of the prohibited grounds.[14]

THE CHILD CARE ACT, 2005

Section 52A of the Child Care Act of 1983 provides that no one may employ or give work to any child under the age of 15 years. The Act was amended by the Child Care Amendment Bill in 1999 to provide for the right to appeal against orders made in the Children's Courts or refusal by the Courts to make an order for the placement of a child in alternative care. The law also empowers the Minister of Justice to establish and maintain facilities for children awaiting trial or sentencing, and to impose severe penalties for sexual exploitation of children. The Bill became the Child Care Act of 2005. The Children Amendment Bill of July 2006 has not altered the section on children's employment.

THE BASIC CONDITIONS OF EMPLOYMENT ACT 75, 1997

Closely linked to the above, Section 43 of the Basic Conditions of Employment Act (BCEA) stipulates that no one may employ a child who is under 15 years of age or who is under the minimum school-leaving age in terms of any law if this is 15 or older. This Act further states that no one may employ a child in employment that is inappropriate for a person of that age and that places at risk a child's wellbeing, education, physical or mental health, or spiritual, moral or social development.

At this stage, it needs to be pointed out that the reasons for child labour go beyond the reach of international, regional and national legal frameworks of oversight and enforcement; behind child labour are social, cultural and historical realities such as poverty, past inequalities and HIV/AIDS. The link between HIV/AIDS and child labour is yet to be empirically established as the literature on the topic is still limited.

THE HIV/AIDS PANDEMIC IN SOUTH AFRICA

The first recorded death from HIV/AIDS-related infection in South Africa was in 1982. Within a decade, the number of recorded AIDS cases had risen to over 1 000 and by the mid 1990s it had reached 10 000. Until 1998, South Africa had one of the fastest expanding epidemics in the world.[15] It was reported that in 2000, AIDS-related illnesses were the leading cause of deaths in hospitals in the country.[16]

It was reported that 10.8% of all South Africans over two years old were living with HIV in 2005. Among those between 15 and 49 years old, the estimated HIV prevalence was 16.2% in 2005.[17] The country is facing a severe HIV/AIDS crisis and it is estimated that South Africa has the highest number of people living with HIV/AIDS in sub-Saharan Africa. Estimates range from 4.3 to 6 million people living with the virus. A Human Sciences Research Council survey estimates that women between the ages of 25 and 29 are at the highest risk of being infected with prevalence rates at 33.3%. The highest overall infection rate is in KwaZulu-Natal with a prevalence rate of 37.5%. In 2005, the World Health Organisation reported that there are 400 000 new infections a year which translate into more than 1 000 new infections daily (Oxfam, 2006: 5). Clearly, HIV/AIDS poses a serious threat to South Africa.

ORPHANS AND VULNERABLE CHILDREN IN SOUTH AFRICA: THE IMPACT ON CHILD LABOUR

Despite significant efforts to ensure the rights of children, most children in South Africa have a difficult start in life. This is due mainly to poverty, inadequate policy support and services, HIV/AIDS, cross-border travel, widespread alcohol and substance abuse, intergenerational sex between older men and young women, ignorance and, in some cases, harmful cultural practices, to name but a few. In addition, HIV/AIDS has weakened and redefined the family structures in Southern Africa and South Africa has not been spared.

The advent of HIV/AIDS in the early 1980s has worsened the disadvantaged position of children in South Africa. HIV/AIDS does not only affect the health of young people. The infection has a huge impact upon children in different ways, ranging from stigmatisation and discrimination to abuse of their basic rights. For young people infected and affected by HIV, the impact of the disease upon their right to survival and development becomes apparent when we consider the extent of orphaning associated with the pandemic (Save the Children, 2001:1). It has been estimated that as a result of AIDS, by 2010 orphans will constitute 9-12% of the South African population. Research also shows that up to 800 000 children in South Africa have lost either their parents or their sole known parent – usually their mother – to AIDS. This figure was expected to reach a million by 2005, climbing as high as three million by 2010 (Desmond & Gow, 2002).

CHILD-HEADED HOUSEHOLDS

As a result of HIV/AIDS, households headed by children are now a recurrent and overwhelming phenomenon in South Africa. This is largely due to the failure and collapse of the extended family. Sadly, in the debate around child-headed house-holds, the issue of gender cannot be ignored. In most cases, child-headed households are run by girls (Mturi & Nzimande, 2003).[18] Moreover, the girl child is more likely to drop out of school to look after her younger siblings.[19] The urge to serve as care-giver often leads girls into risky sexual behaviour and increases the already vulnera-ble position of females vis-à-vis HIV/AIDS.

In short, children in South Africa today are faced with two predicaments: Firstly, they have to deal with HIV infection and AIDS illness. Secondly, in the event they are not themselves infected or ill, they may be forced to work to fulfil parenting duties in caring for sick siblings.[20]

HIV/AIDS is therefore intensifying the problem of child labour. This has been well documented by the Commission reviewing the Child Care Act of 1983. The extent of child labour resulting from AIDS orphaning is yet to be fully investigated but it stands to reason that children may be undertaking jobs that are harmful to their health and moral development.

This is supported by the fact that even though child labour is prohibited by law, it has been widespread in informal and agricultural sectors, particularly in the former homeland areas. The government generally enforces child labour laws in the formal sectors of the economy, while the informal sectors tend to be more difficult to regulate.

The UN Committee on the Rights of the Child, in its concluding observations fol-lowing the South African report in 2000, noted that the country has signed a memo-randum of understanding with the ILO's International Programme for the Elimination of Child Labour to undertake a national survey to compile comprehen-sive national child labour statistics.

The UN Committee was concerned that over 200 000 children between the age of 10 and 14 were engaged in work, mainly commercial agriculture and domestic service.[21] In its concluding observations, the UN Committee also expressed its concern about the high and increasing incidence of HIV/AIDS and STDs.

THE HUMAN RIGHTS DISCOURSE

It is argued that, in reviewing the relatively short history of responses to the HIV/AIDS pandemic, a common denominator of effective programmes is the respect for human rights and dignity of persons. HIV/AIDS is therefore a human rights issue that has to be approached by applying human rights principles (M.E Wojcik, cited in Gumedze, 2004).

CHILDREN'S RIGHTS AS HUMAN RIGHTS

Recently we have seen a move away from a discourse on children's needs to one on children's rights.[22] The Vienna Declaration and Plan of Action[23] derives from the principle that human rights and fundamental freedoms are the birthright of all human beings. Based upon the premise that all human rights are universal, indivisible and interrelated, the Vienna Declaration further states that the international community must treat human rights globally in a fair and equal manner, on the same footing, and with the same emphasis... "it is the duty of states, regardless of their political, economic and cultural systems, to promote and protect all human rights and fundamental freedoms".[24] The Preamble of the United Nations Declaration of the Rights of the Child[25] reiterates the fundamental rights of the child while Article 27 of the CRC reinforces the same rights.

The legal status of international instruments will differ from country to country but international human rights instruments have an indisputable moral force and are legally binding on their signatories. To this effect, section 231(2) of the South African Constitution states that:

> An international agreement binds the Republic only after it has been approved by resolution in both the National Assembly and the National Council of Provinces, unless it is an agreement referred to in subsection (3).

For its part, the African Charter on Human and Peoples' Rights states in Article 2 that:

> Every individual shall be entitled to the enjoyment of the rights and freedoms recognized and guaranteed in the present charter without distinction of any kind such as race, ethnic group, colour, sex, language, religion, political or any other opinion, national and social origin, fortune, birth or other status.

Given the above, the question that follows is how to reconcile the human rights discourse with the issues of child labour generated by HIV/AIDS.

One of the most effective way to combat the spread of HIV/AIDS is through the protection of people living with the virus, and those around them, from discrimination. This may appear to be a paradox because many communities expect laws to protect the uninfected from the infected (Kirby, quoted in Prinsloo & Beckman, 2003: 318-319).

We need to consider that the concept of "rights" is relatively new in South Africa, and people do not always take advantage of all the rights available for their protection for a variety of reasons, including illiteracy and lack of information. It is even less likely that children will understand the concepts of "rights" and "children's rights" particularly if they cannot access the school system. It is therefore a major challenge to the state to ensure that information, education and communication campaigns are put in place and sustained so that all citizens, including the youngest and most vulnerable, are informed of their rights and responsibilities.

South Africa is a country endowed with immense resources and is quite capable of turning this around. There are indications that 12 years after the end of apartheid, a rights culture is clearly under way and South Africa has been able to work with a host of international agencies, including a range of UN organisations such as UNICEF and UNAIDS and the World Health Organisation (WHO), gaining enormously from their support and expertise, to tackle critical and emerging issues.

THE CORE PRINCIPLES
We need to delve deeper into the core principles of children's rights as laid down in the CRC and the African Charter. These principles embrace all the other rights enshrined in the UN instruments and provide guidance to nation-states in terms of their application. Since the Teheran Proclamation of 1968, the interrelatedness and interdependency of human rights have been reinforced in various international declarations and conventions. The CRC underscores four core principles relating to children's rights. These principles lie at the heart of the CRC and are discussed below.

THE BEST INTEREST PRINCIPLE
Section 28(2) of the South African Constitution, Article 3(1) of the CRC, Article 4 of the ACRWC and Articles 16(1) (d) and (f) of the UN Convention on the Elimination of All Forms of Discrimination against Women enshrine the "best interests of the child" standard as the "paramount" or "primary" consideration in all matters concerning children. However, it has been argued that the "best interests" standard is problematic in that, inter alia, (i) it is "indeterminate"; (ii) the different professionals involved with matters relating to children have different perspectives on the concept; and (iii) the way in which the criterion is interpreted and applied by different countries (and, indeed, by different courts and other decision-makers within the same country) is influenced to a large extent by the historical background to, and the cultural, social, political and economic conditions of, the country concerned.

NON-DISCRIMINATION
Experience has shown that children both infected and affected by HIV/AIDS are still subjected to traumatic stigmatisation and discrimination from a wide range of sectors, including the health care, educational and welfare sectors, and more disturbingly, from their own communities and extended families. Discrimination may be defined by employing three equations. It has been equated with action (McCrudden, 1991: xivff):
• Motivated by prejudice or "discriminatory intent";
• Motivated by factors other than prejudice; or

- Which has the effect of disproportionately disadvantaging a particular group defined by sex or race, yet which cannot be justified by other countervailing considerations.[26]

In the Equality Act, "discrimination" is defined in such broad terms that it includes indirect discrimination such as:

> *any act or omission, including a policy, law, rule, practice, condition or situation, which directly or indirectly (a) imposes burdens, obligations or disadvantage on; or (b) withholds benefits, opportunities or advantages from, any person on one or more prohibited grounds.*[27]

Although the laws exist to prevent discrimination on the basis of HIV/AIDS status, the reality is that they often cannot be enforced, partly due to lack of knowledge on basic human rights and limited state outreach.

PARTICIPATION

In a general sense, the government and state institutions supporting democracy are actively involving children in participatory processes in South Africa. For instance, children actively participated in the South African Law Commission's consultations in the review of the Child Care Act and the establishment of a juvenile justice system. In the same vein, the Schools Act of 1996 explicitly calls for active participation of children in school governing bodies. Children now have a say in how their schools are run. Children, as full members of governing bodies, have the same rights as both parents and teachers in terms of voting and the right to be heard.[28] However, child labour in South Africa continues unabated and children's voices are still subdued.

SURVIVAL AND DEVELOPMENT

With HIV/AIDS undermining children's ability to grow up within an environment which can meet their basic physical, emotional, social and education needs and fulfil their right to family or family-like care, survival and development rights are increasingly challenged. The following categories of children are identified as AIDS-affected children in need of special protection: children in households in which one or other members are infected with HIV or AIDS; children orphaned by AIDS; children who are HIV-positive or have AIDS; and abandoned infants.[29] Children born with HIV or those who are AIDS orphans face immediate and grave obstacles to establish their own humanity (Viljoen, 2003: 215). While young people are at the centre of the epidemic's transmission and impact, they are certainly not at the centre of the resource allocation (Dick, Ferguson & Ross, 2006: 10).

SOUTH AFRICA'S COMPLIANCE WITH ITS INTERNATIONAL AND REGIONAL OBLIGATIONS

In September 1990, the World Summit for Children, comprising a record number of world leaders, was held in New York to give the highest level of political endorsement to the survival, development and protection of the rights of all children "without discrimination of any kind" in line with article 2 of the CRC. The Convention also formally recognised the role of families as the natural and primary protectors of children's rights, but underscored the obligation of states to support families to enable them to fulfil their responsibilities.[30]

The preamble of the CRC in accordance with the principles proclaimed in the UN Charter[31] recognises that the inherent dignity and the equal and inalienable rights of all members of the human family are the foundations of freedom, justice and peace in the world. The preamble further recognises that the UN has, in the Universal Declaration of Human Rights[32] and in the international covenants on human rights,[33] proclaimed and agreed that everyone is entitled to all the rights and freedoms set forth therein, without distinction of any kind, such as race, colour, sex, language, religion, political or other opinion, national or social origin, property, birth or other status.

Article 43 of the CRC establishes a Committee on the Rights of the Child. The purpose of the Committee is to examine the progress made by states in achieving the obligations undertaken in the CRC. Article 44 states that:

> 1. State Parties undertake to submit to the Committee, through the Secretary-General of the United Nations, reports on the measures they have adopted which give effect to the rights recognized herein and on the progress made on the enjoyment of those rights:
>   (a) Within two years of the entry into force of the Convention for the State Party concerned;
>   (b) Thereafter every five years.
> 2. Reports made under the present article shall indicate factors and difficulties, if any, affecting the degree of fulfilment of the obligations under the present Convention.

Reports must also contain sufficient information to provide the Committee with a comprehensive understanding of the implementation of the CRC in the country concerned.

For its part, the ACRWC is based on the Declaration on the Rights and Welfare of the African Child, 1979,[34] which recognises the need to take appropriate measures to promote and protect the rights and welfare of the African Child. Article 32 of the ACRWC established an African Committee of Experts on the Rights and Welfare of the child within the African Union. The Committee's functions are to promote and protect the rights enshrined in the ACRWC and in particular to collect and document information, commission inter-disciplinary assessment of problems in Africa regarding the rights and welfare of the child, organise meetings, formulate and lay down principles and rules aimed at protecting the rights and welfare of children in Africa and cooperate with other African, international and regional institutions and organisations.

In terms of article 43 of the ACRWC, each state party to the ACRWC must report to the African Committee on measures adopted and progress made in implementing the ACRWC. State parties should submit the initial report within two years of the entry into force of the ACRWC for the state party concerned and every three years thereafter.

In contrast to the UN CRC, the African Committee is authorised by the Charter to receive complaints against state parties concerning any issue covered by the instrument from any individual, group or non-governmental organisation (NGO) recognised by the AU or the UN.[35]

REPORTING TO THE COMMITTEE ON THE RIGHTS OF THE CHILD AND TO THE COMMITTEE OF EXPERTS ON THE RIGHTS AND WELFARE OF THE CHILD.

THE COMMITTEE ON THE RIGHTS OF THE CHILD AND SOUTH AFRICA

As stated earlier, South Africa ratified the CRC immediately after the advent of democracy in June 1995. South Africa submitted its initial country report in 1997, and it was considered in 2000. The Committee noted some positive aspects in the report, such as the enactment of legislation to bring about a greater harmonisation between domestic laws and the CRC. Furthermore, the implementation of the National Programme of Action was welcomed. The launching of a Children's Budget Project with the aim of developing an overall perspective on the government's expenditure on children's programmes and examining the impact of this expenditure on the lives of children was also welcomed.

However, overcoming the legacy of apartheid continues to have a negative impact on the situation of children and to impede the full implementation of the CRC. The vast economic and social disparities that continue between various segments of society as well as the relatively high levels of unemployment and poverty which adversely affect the full implementation of the CRC remain challenges for South Africa.

THE COMMITTEE OF EXPERTS ON THE RIGHTS AND WELFARE OF THE CHILD AND SOUTH AFRICA

The Department of Social Development has the responsibility to ensure the welfare of all children in South Africa, and it therefore has a mandate to compile the report. Its partners in this are the Department of Education, the Department of Health, the Department of Justice, NGOs and UN structures. Information on children's issues should be collected from various stakeholders in the country and the report compiled under the supervision of the Department. In drafting the report, different stakeholders must be consulted.

The African Committee of Experts has also compiled guidelines for initial reports of state parties.[36] Although South Africa ratified the ACRWC in 2000 no report has been submitted yet.

CONCLUSION

The causes of child labour extend beyond the lack of a legal and regulatory framework and enforcement to complex social, cultural and economic factors. HIV/AIDS is fast becoming foremost among these factors. Compared to other human rights instruments, every single convention pertaining to children's rights has been ratified by almost all UN member states. The challenge remains to translate this commitment into actions favouring children worldwide, especially those infected/affected by HIV/AIDS and who are forced to enter the labour market prematurely as a result.

REFERENCES

Desmond, C. & Gow, J. (eds.) 2002. *Impacts and Interventions: The HIV/AIDS Epidemic and the Children in South Africa.* Pietermaritzburg: University of KwaZulu-Natal Press.

Dick, B., Ferguson, J. & Ross, D.A. (eds.) 2006. "Preventing HIV/AIDS in Young People: A Systematic Review of the Evidence from Developing Countries," UNAIDS Inter-Agency Task Team on Young People

Gumedze, S. 2004. "HIV/AIDS and Human Rights: The Role of the African Commission on Human and Peoples' Rights," *African Human Rights Law Journal,* 4.

Jagwanth, S. & Kalula, E. (eds.) 2001. *Equality Law: Reflections from South Africa and Elsewhere.* Cape Town: Juta Law.

Jayawickrama, N. 2002. *The Judicial Application of the Human Rights Law: National, Regional and International Jurisprudence.* Cambridge: Cambridge University Press.

McCrudden, C. (ed.) 1991. *Anti-Discrimination Law.* Aldershot: Dartmouth Publishing.

Mturi, A. & Nzimande, N. 2003. *HIV/AIDS and Child Labour in South Africa: A Rapid Assessment: The Case Study of Kwazulu Natal.* Geneva: International Labour Organisation, International Programme on the Elimination of Child Labour, Paper 4.

Oxfam, 2006. *Essential Services: HIV, Health Services and Gender in South Africa: A Report by Oxfam International.* South Africa: Oxfam.

Prinsloo, J. & Beckman, J. 2003. "HIV/AIDS and the Learner," in Davel, C.J. (ed.) *Introduction to Child Law in South Africa.* Cape Town: Juta Law.

Save the Children, 2001. *Children, HIV/AIDS and the Law: A Legal Resource.* Save the Children, South Africa programme.

Shadrack, G, 2001. *Equality and Non-Discrimination in South Africa: The Political Economy of Law and Law Making.* Cape Town: New Africa Books.

South African Law Commission, Review of the Child Care Act 1983, xlviii.

Steinbock, B. 2006. "Defining Parenthood," in Freeman, M. (ed.) *Children's Health and Children's Rights.* Leiden: Martinus Nijhoff Publishers.

Terreblanche, S. 2002. *A History of Inequality in South Africa 1652-2002.* Pietermaritzburg: University of KwaZulu-Natal Press and KMM Review Publishing.

Viljoen, F. 2003. "The African Charter on the Rights and Welfare of the Child," in Davel, C.J. (ed.) *Introduction to Child Law in South Africa.* Cape Town: Juta Law.

Zehra, A. 2002. "Analyzing Child Labor as a Human Rights Issue: Its Causes, Aggravating Policies and Alternative Proposals," *Human Rights Quarterly,* I, 177-204.

---

1 The CRC was adopted and opened for signature, ratification and accession by General Assembly Resolution 44/25 of 20 November 1989, and entered into force on 2 September 1990, in accordance with Article 49.

2 The United States has signalled its intention to ratify the convention — but has yet to do so. Somalia is currently unable to ratify the CRC because it lacks a recognised government. See UNICEF, "Frequently Asked Questions," available at: http://www.unicef.org/crc/faq.htm#009 accessed 3 October 2006.

3 See www.embassy.org.nz/encycl/c2encyc.htm accessed 27 September 2006

4 See www.childlaborphotoproject.org/childlabor.html accessed 27 September 2006.

5 Ibid.

6 See article 7 of the ILO Minimum Age Convention. In other words, this section says that children between 12 and 15 years may engage in economic activities that are not harmful to them. This includes activities such as distribution of newspapers before school.

7 See Article 1 of the ILO Worst Forms of Child Labour Convention, 1999.

8 The ACRWC, OAU Doc. CAB/LEG/24.9/49 (1990), entered into force on 29 November 1999.

9 The Assembly of Heads of State and Government is composed of heads of state and government or their duly accredited representatives. The Assembly is the supreme organ of the African Union.

10 The African Charter on Human and Peoples' Rights, adopted on 27 June 1981, OAU Doc. CAB/LEG/3, rev. 5, 21 I.L.M. 58 (1982), entered into force on 21 October 1986.

11 See the Preamble to the African Charter.

12 Declaration on the Rights and Welfare of the African Child, AHG/ST.4 Rev.l, adopted by the Assembly of Heads of State and Government of the Organisation of African Unity at its Sixteenth Ordinary Session in Monrovia, Liberia, 17 to 20 July 1979.

13 See also para. 3, preamble of the Equality Act.

14 Chapter 1, art (1) viii of the Promotion of Equality and the Prevention of Unfair Discrimination Act 4 of 2000.

15 South African HIV/AIDS statistics available at www.avert.org/safricastast.htm accessed 18 September 2006.

16 "AIDS-Related Illnesses Leading Cause of Death in South Africa in 2000, Medical Research Council Report Says," at www.medicalnewstoday.com/medicalnews.php?newsid=24680#top accessed 20 September 2006.

17 Ibid.

18 Available at http://sds.ukzn.ac.za/default.php? 7,6,232,4,0 accessed 19 September 2006.

19 Ibid.

20 South Africa Country Reports on Human Rights Practices – 2005. Released by the Bureau of Democracy, Human Rights and Labour, March 8, 2006 http://www.state.gov/g/drl/rls/hrrpt/2005/61593.htm accessed 20 September 2006.

21 Concluding Observations of the Committee on the Rights of the Child, South Africa, UN Doc. CRC/C/15/Add.122 (2000).

22 "Children, HIV/AIDS and the Law, A Legal Resource." A project of the National AIDS and Children Task Team (NACTT), commissioned by Save the Children UK South Africa Programme. Available at http://www.childrensrightscentre.co.za/legal_audit/DocSum.htm accessed 20 September 2006.

23 Vienna Declaration and Plan of Action adopted at the World Conference on Human Rights, Vienna 14-25 June 1993, UN General Assembly doc A/CONF 137/23.

24 Ibid, para 5.

25 Declaration of the Rights on the Child proclaimed by General Assembly resolution 1386(XIV) of 20 November 1959.

26 In South Africa, when courts consider an equality claim the primary issue is the impact of the discrimination, and not whether it treats different groups identically: S. Liebenberg & M. O'Sullivan, see "South Africa's New Equality Legislation: A Tool for Advancing Women's Socio-economic Equality'. in: Jagwanth, Saras & Kalula, Evance (eds.). 2001: 70-103, at p.78; also N. Jayawickrama, 2002; and G. Shadrack, 2001: 127.

27 Section 1(1)(viii), sv "discrimination," Equality Act.

28 Minister Essop Pahad, opening remarks at the UN Committee on the Rights of the Child, Geneva, Switzerland, 25 January 2000. Presentation of the South Africa Country Progress Report on the Implementation of the Convention on the Rights of the Child, available at http://www.gcis.gov.za/media/minister/000125.htm accessed 20 September 2006.

29 Review of the Child Care Act 1983 by the South African Law Commission, xlviii.

30 See Preamble and Article 18 respectively of the CRC.

31 The Charter of the United Nations signed at San Francisco on 26 June 1945 entered into force 24 October 1945 in accordance with Article 110.

32 Universal Declaration of Human Rights, adopted and proclaimed by General Assembly Resolution 217 A (iii) of 10 December 1948.

33 The International Covenant on Civil and Political Rights, 1966 and the International Covenant on Economic, Social and Cultural Rights, 1966. South Africa has not ratified the International Covenant on Economic, Social and Cultural Rights.

34 Declaration on the Rights and Welfare of the African Child, AHG/ST.4 Rev.l, adopted by the Assembly of Heads of State and Government of the Organisation of African Unity, at its Sixteenth Ordinary Session in Monrovia, Liberia. 17-20 July 1979.

35 See article 44 of the ACRWC.

36 These guidelines are available at http://www.africa-union.org/child/home.htm accessed 4 October 2006.

CHAPTER 5

CHILDREN'S EXPERIENCES OF THE LINK BETWEEN POVERTY AND UNEMPLOYMENT IN THE CONTEXT OF HIV/AIDS

DEBORAH EWING

"Dear Mr President
I am Lettie, I am 14 years old. I wrote this letter to you, as we are children we ask you
to help us to stay with our family. Help the children on the street, give them enough
care and love. Can you please give our family money and give them jobs so that they
can feed us enough food.
Yours Faithfully
Lettie"[1]

INTRODUCTION

The child who wrote this letter was staying in a temporary home for girls at risk of
ending up on the streets due to food insecurity, poor health status, exclusion from
school, neglect (resulting from parental absence and stress) and exposure to substance abuse and violence. All the 18 children had parents and had previously lived
in their family's home but their families were unable to meet their basic needs
because of poverty and unemployment.

Children are generally (and appropriately) dependent on adults to meet their
material and some of their emotional needs. Therefore, the material and emotional
circumstances of the adults they live with directly affect the quality of life of the
child. The majority of children experience poverty as members of families or households rather than as individuals. Therefore, the inability of the household to sustain
itself impacts directly on the survival and development of the child. Children are
acutely aware of this and talk about poverty in terms of the status of their parents
or family.[2]

Before looking at children's specific observations about poverty, it is important to
recognise the chronic nature of poverty in South Africa.[3] Children here, as in many
other countries, are *inheriting poverty*. For many households, poverty is not a temporary cash-flow crisis but an ongoing, intergenerational state of deprivation. Children
are born into and grow up in households where no one has a living wage. Obviously
this has its roots in the deliberate subjugation and exclusion of black South Africans
under colonialism and apartheid but the impacts of economic globalisation and
HIV/AIDS have perpetuated this long-term poverty.

The unemployment and limited employment opportunities of parents or other
caregivers are passed on to children. Children and young people from Stellenbosch
and from Wentworth, Durban,[4] described how their prospects for escaping poverty
through employment, as well as their expectations of finding work and their career
aspirations were shaped by the experiences of their parents. For example, one young
man spoke of how children saw no alternative to following in the footsteps of their
fathers – to be a panel beater in Durban or work at a refinery or on a construction
site in the Western Cape. Several children saw that their escape route from poverty
required doing something completely different from their parents but felt even
education would not make that possible.

CHILDREN'S EXPERIENCE OF POVERTY AND UNEMPLOYMENT

Children experience poverty as multi-dimensional, not solely related to lack of income but also to insecurity, vulnerability, exclusion and loss of hope.

Despite their different backgrounds and situations, all the children interviewed defined poverty in a very broad and multi-faceted way. Their definitions included income poverty and lack of material resources but also social and emotional dimensions – such as shame, fear and insecurity, loss of hope and exclusion.

The link between exclusion and socialisation has serious implications. A group of children of farmworkers said that the problems facing children living in poverty included family tension – "they fight a lot" – and social difficulties – "they do not have enough friends".

Children know that rights are "indivisible" – that the rights to food, shelter, family, health, education and other essentials are not hierarchical but inter-dependent.

One of the groups of orphaned children who did a budget allocation activity expressed this by earmarking equal amounts for education and food – "because you can't go to school on an empty stomach, so the two things go together".
Children do not see rights in isolation from each other, or in a hierarchy. All their needs have to be met. The United Nation's Convention on the Rights of the Child identifies four pillars of children's rights – survival, protection, development and participation.

Clearly South Africa is failing badly on the first count. Official data from the Western Cape show that among children in Khayelitsha under five years old the most prevalent causes of death relate to preventable and treatable conditions, such as HIV/AIDS (22%), diarrhoea (13%) and pneumonia (12%). Children are literally dying from poverty; in households where there is adequate income children are less likely to become sick and are treated if they do.

Protection and development require the realisation of children's rights to family, health and welfare services, education, recreation and justice. There is a whole range of barriers to achieving this but lack of income means that most other rights cannot be enjoyed because they all involve payment for fees and/or transport. The right to participate in decision-making is widely viewed at best as a luxury and at worst as some Northern-imposed irrelevance. Participation is often understood by adults to mean "presence" or opportunities to dance or sing. Children's right to express views and concerns that may inform and enrich anti-poverty and development strategies is rarely recognised.

In the context of poverty and unemployment, children's rights are "traded off" – children enjoy one basic right only at the expense of another. This is exacerbated by the impoverishing effects of HIV/AIDS.

The lack of income, reduced opportunities and poor access to services that result from unemployment mean that caregivers are unable to meet all children's basic needs. Children suffer greatly when their rights have to be traded off against each other. Their right to food may be traded for the right to education; the right to education traded for the right to family; the right to family traded for the right to leisure time (because of the need to look after siblings). The children in the girls' home had all their basic socioeconomic needs met at the expense of their right to family life, which they all, without exception, saw as a terrible loss, despite the suffering they might have experienced at home (Ewing, 2004).

In the context of HIV/AIDS and other causes of orphanhood, labour migrancy and abandonment, millions of children are not living with their biological parents.[5] The majority have been absorbed into their wider families or into households to which they are not related, which now have to spread their limited resources more thinly. This not only exacerbates the material poverty of children but their vulnerability and lack of opportunities.

A Save the Children Fund study in Malawi found that orphaned children would prefer to live with a loving granny in poverty than with a well-off relative who did not care for them (Mann, 2004). That is an important consideration when arranging alternative care in a crisis but it should not be the basis for planning policy and budgeting responses in line with the Bill of Rights. We should be planning for children to live in a loving family environment *and* to have all their material needs met. And we should be listening to children's assessment of how this is best done.

Children want their parents and families to be able to take care of them – and want the government to fulfil its constitutional duty to support households that cannot do this.

Many of the children interviewed in a study by the Institute for Democracy in South Africa (IDASA) saw their rights in relation to the ability of caregivers to meet their needs (Ewing, 2004). When they set their budget priorities, the imperative for the state to bridge the gap between children's socioeconomic rights and support for families/households came through very clearly. Children were very aware of the difficulties their parents faced in trying to look after them. Employment and decent wages – for their parents or themselves in the case of child-headed households – were commonly seen as urgent needs, rather than the goods and services that could be bought as a result.[6] Children did not share the symptomatic approach to poverty alleviation of some policy-makers and economists.

The top priority of children who had all their basic needs met but did not live at home was to be reunited with their families. When asked what *their most urgent needs were, as individuals* they spoke about what *their parents needed* to be able to look after them – primarily an income and a home.

The children were asked what they thought the government should do to reduce poverty among children. Many, like Lettie in her letter above, wrote to the president expressing their needs. Here are a few of their requests:

> "We as children want better lives and not [to] stay on the street, and we want...to go back to our families. Some of our families don't have good jobs and we hope that you can help us."

> "I am asking for help because I want to study but my parents are poor. My mother isn't working and my father has gone. You are helping other children at home [with grants], including one who is disabled..."

> "...please can you give my mother a house to stay in with me?"

One group of children said if they were Minister of Finance Trevor Manuel their priority would be to ensure that parents "earn more money".

> *Children in impoverished and HIV/AIDS-affected households do not want to be objects of charity and pity.*

Children do not want handouts from neighbours, religious bodies or from the government. They want their families to be able to take care of them. Children have said it distresses them that their next meal comes from a charity or a feeding scheme because their parents cannot provide for them. Indeed some children would rather go hungry than accept a meal that is part of the school feeding programme and let people see they do not get fed at home.[7] Children have a right to a family and to have their basic physical needs met. In the event that their parents cannot take care of them, the state has a duty to assist.[8] Where children are in families, that duty should relate to the family. Surely parents have a right, as well as a duty, to provide for their children and to be assisted to do so.

Given the dire circumstances of more than half the nation's children, there is a need for urgent welfare assistance *alongside* longer-term livelihood support. But children want to see that channelled through their caregivers. A Basic Income Grant would be one approach to giving households the means to provide for their children. The "dependency" argument against this really doesn't hold water – social grant recipients are no more dependent on their grants than the Minister of Finance is on his salary. Research by the Economic Policy Research Institute in its 2004 study of the impact of social grants has shown that grants give people a chance to become less dependent by enabling them to feed themselves, to travel to seek work or to start a micro-enterprise. Children expect to be dependent on their parents and research with children about how grants enable adults to meet children's basic needs would be valuable.

Children feel poverty most keenly in relation to inequality – the pain of suffering more or less than other children adds to the objective measures of poverty.

A group of girls in Cape Town, all from extremely income-poor homes, insisted that they were not poor – because poor people were homeless and begged on the streets and that was shameful. Children of farmworkers in Stellenbosch spoke of being teased in school by educators and peers because they came from the farm. "Children are treated differently when they are poor," said the child of a farmworker.

These children initially denied living in poverty but when they conceded that their living conditions were poor, they qualified this by saying they were "spiritually rich". They denied going hungry but were able to explain in graphic detail what it felt like to go to bed without food.

Many of the children interviewed said that children as a group suffered most from poverty. This is not only true in numerical terms in South Africa; it is also true in terms of the immediacy of the impact of poverty. Children are hungry now and kept out of school now and they lack the means to improve their circumstances. The full range of impacts on children is not generally considered.

One group of primary school children *defined* poverty as: "kinders wat swaar kry' "(children who suffer/fall on hard times.) This supports the case for policy and budgeting responses that address child poverty in a comprehensive way that takes account of children's experiences.

RECOGNITION OF CHILDREN'S EXPERIENCE

Children are not passive victims of the deadly triangle of poverty, unemployment and HIV/AIDS but are active in household coping strategies.

The children interviewed shared not only their experiences of poverty and their assessment of their most pressing needs but also their ideas of what should be done to address those needs.

In several cases children interviewed in the IDASA study were taking over responsibility for meeting everyone's needs. One direct consequence of adult unemployment is that children are taken out of school (notwithstanding "free" education) and sometimes end up working to support the household. In Msinga, for example, a sister and brother had left school and were working to support an extended family of several adults and children – but were still left out of decision-making about household spending and resource allocation.

Research in many countries shows that "children can have the ability not only to determine their own lives but to also influence those of others" (Boyden, *et al.*, 2003: 85). Aside from the household chores and the caregiving they perform, children's contributions enable many families to survive. One study of nine Latin American countries found that without the income of children aged between 13 and 17 the incidence of poverty (as measured by the absolute poverty line) would rise by 10-20%.[9]

> *The role of children in households trapped in this triangle is not recognised or understood in most planning, programming and budgeting.*

While recent policy prescribes an holistic approach to meeting the needs of vulnerable children, it tends not to recognise the agency of children. Economic policy does not reflect children's needs for an integrated social benefit/income support and livelihood strategy.

> *The ideas and insights of children about measures needed to address a crisis that affects them most acutely are rarely sought or considered.*

There are few opportunities for children's voices to be heard other than through once-off events. It tends to be only older children whose views are sought even though non-governmental organisations have experience of participatory research with young children. A paper based on research for the Bernard van Leer Foundation[10] to identify responses to meet the needs of children aged 0-8 living in HIV/AIDS-affected communities highlighted gaps at local, national and international levels in programming and policy. It said that services were urgently required to support very young children both directly and through the families and communities in which they live and that "ways of listening to and including very young children in these processes need to be developed and used".[11]

PRIORITIES FOR RESEARCHING CHILDREN'S EXPERIENCE

Many of the points discussed above come from the findings of research that focused on whether the basic socioeconomic needs of particularly vulnerable children were being met. It did not focus particularly on who was meeting those needs or how the children felt about the provision. Nevertheless the children's views on these issues came out very strongly. A range of issues require further participatory, preferably action, research with children. These include:

- Children's perceptions of the causes and effects of poverty and unemployment;
- Children's role in supporting households and mitigating the effects of household poverty;
- The implications of children's experience for social cohesion and future citizenship;
- The impact of caregiver unemployment on relationships between adults and children;
- Children's experience of child-focused social grants – including the impact on quality of life, the impact on relationships and their assessment of spending choices made by caregivers;
- Children's views of the support their families need and how it should be provided.

REFERENCES

Boyden, J., Eyber, C., Feeny, T. & Scott, C. 2003. *Children and Poverty. Voices of Children: Experiences and Perceptions from Belarus, Bolivia, India, Kenya and Sierra Leone.* Children and Poverty Series part 2. Christian Children's Fund.

De Swardt, K. 2003. *Unravelling Chronic Poverty in South Africa: Some Food for Thought.* Cape Town: University of Cape Town.

Ewing, D. 2004. *Report on the Children's Participation Component of Monitoring Child Socio-Economic Rights in South Africa: Achievements and Challenges.* Cape Town: IDASA.

Mann, G. 2004. *Family Matters: the Care and Protection of Children Affected by HIV/AIDS in Malawi.* Stockholm: Save the Children.

1 Excerpt from a letter to the president written by a child living in a shelter in Cape Town.
2 These children and three other groups of children living in difficult circumstances took part in workshops on how far their basic needs were being met and what they thought needed to be done when they were not. They included children in a remote rural area of KwaZulu-Natal, child heads of household and their siblings in townships near Pietermaritzburg and children of farmworkers around Stellenbosch.
3 See the work of the Chronic Poverty Research Centre (www.chronicpoverty.org.za), especially Kobus de Swardt. 2003. *Unravelling Chronic Poverty in South Africa: Some Food for Thought.* Cape Town: University of Cape Town.
4 Author's interviews with children during a careers guidance workshop (2004) and input from young people on role models as part of the Fatherhood Project (2004), an initiative of the Human Sciences Research Council aimed at encouraging men's involvement in the care and protection of children and highlighting the role of men as care-givers using various forms of media. A second, long-term aim is to develop a research agenda on father-child issues.
5 According to UNAIDS, a total of 2.2 million children in South Africa, that is 13% of all children, had lost either a mother or father by 2003. About 1 million of those children are estimated to have lost parents due to AIDS.
6 Multi-country research with children reflects this. A study of children and poverty asked "What are the main causes of poverty in your country?" and "unemployment" was the top answer. See Boyden, *et al.*
7 Interviews with children of farmworkers in the Western Cape (see Ewing, 2004), interviews with educators in KwaZulu-Natal (author's research for an impact assessment for the Children's Rights Centre, Durban, in 2002) and interviews with care workers from Muthande Society for the Aged, Durban, 2005.
8 UN Convention on the Rights of the Child. Article 27, Section 3.
9 Unicef 1997. Cited in Christian Children's Fund, 2003.
10 "HIV/AIDS: What about very young children?" Available at http://www.healthcomms.org/resource/find2-key.html
11 Save the Children Fund United Kingdom has developed a resource kit on children's participation in orphans and vulnerable children programming.

CHAPTER 6

HOW DO CHILD CARE AND CHILD CARE RELATIONSHIPS OPERATE IN THE CONTEXT OF UNEMPLOYMENT AND HIV/AIDS?

RACHEL BRAY AND RENÉ BRANDT

A FOCUS ON CARE: FILLING A GAP IN KNOWLEDGE ABOUT EMPLOYMENT, HIV AND CHILDREN

Much of the work to date on the effect of employment scarcity and HIV on children in southern Africa focuses on demographic change following AIDS-related morbidity and mortality, as well as household-level responses to these changes.

Research in Lesotho has shown increased mobility of adults and children and the resultant fragmentation of households (Young and Ansell, 2003). In South Africa a study encompassing six rural and urban areas that looked at the needs of and supports available to orphaned and other vulnerable children found that HIV/AIDS largely exacerbated the effects of chronic and extreme poverty (Giese et al., 2003). Further, a small but growing body of work looks at state attempts to resource poor children in a climate of unemployment and HIV/AIDS (Leatt et al., 2005). One such study shows the negative implications of directing state social assistance towards orphans rather than the larger proportion of children rendered vulnerable by poverty and HIV/AIDS (Meintjes et al., 2003).

Consistent with the kinds of approaches used in research into employment and HIV, the focus of academic inquiry and policy attention to child care in southern Africa has tended to be limited to analysing household composition and dependency ratios and using these to assess the availability of adults to care for children. Amid the contemporary policy prioritisation of the so-called "crisis of care" and the needs of orphans and children made vulnerable by HIV/AIDS, an unforeseen consequence has been the relatively minimal attention paid to the nature of care (Mann, 2001; 2002; REPPSI, 2003; Richter, Manegold & Pather, 2004; Snider, 2003; Tolfree, 2003; UNAIDS/UNICEF,[1] 2004).

Models of child care developed by international organisations prior to the HIV/AIDS pandemic are of limited use because they tend to posit certain essential components of good quality care, the majority of which centre on practical provision and effectively sideline the interpersonal and emotional dimensions of care (Engle et al., 1997). Further, while anthropological research on South African childhoods offers a more nuanced picture of the normative, economic and socio-political contexts in which care is being performed, it does not attend to the particular considerations and experiences of care relationships (see Henderson, 1999; Jones, 1993; Ramphele, 2002; Reynolds, 1989).

Ethnographic study of child care in other parts of Africa, however, has shown that child care is a complex and dynamic phenomenon, precisely because it is situated in constantly evolving relationships within and beyond the family (Gottlieb, 2004). Moreover, care-giving and other relationships between family members do not persist unresourced, but must be fed with a range of material, social and emotional inputs (Reynolds, 1995). Thus care, at the level of everyday interactions between young children, their relatives, household members and neighbours, is both complex and multi-dimensional.

Further, we know that child care is significant to child wellbeing and therefore of interest to researchers precisely because it has both present and future implications.

Psychologists agree that the quality of children's care relationships – particularly early relationships with primary carers – is an important predictor of child developmental outcomes, often serving as a key factor protecting children from risks associated with living in impoverished communities, including high levels of parental and community unemployment (Bauman *et al.*, 2002; Forehand *et al.*, 2002; Shonkoff and Meisels, 2000). Interestingly, research attention is largely oriented towards these future implications in that most work investigates child "outcomes" (educational, psychosocial or developmental), while studies of current care scenarios tend to look at the absence of care, or "child neglect", or at violence and abuse (Richter *et al.*, 2004).

However, missing from this valuable body of work is knowledge about how the everyday care of children is affected by changes in individual capacities and interpersonal relationships within domestic groups associated with different employment scenarios and AIDS in the home. Thus, our chapter makes a contribution in two important ways: first, in its focus on the details of care-related decisions and actions within the home, and second, in its prioritisation of children's present lived experiences rather than their future outcomes.

RESEARCH APPROACH AND SETTING
Rather than providing detailed information regarding the studies on which this chapter draws, we will restrict ourselves to those comments necessary to situate our discussion points within the relevant socioeconomic and cultural context.[2] Although taking place in various sites in the South Peninsula and Cape Flats area, all communities of interest were representative of several poor settlements in the Cape Town area in which unemployment and underemployment are features in a landscape of poverty and insecurity characterised by a high degree of flux. Available Census data indicate that about half of the economically active population in these areas is unemployed (City of Cape Town, 2006), with the large majority of individual and household incomes falling below thresholds typically considered indicative of poverty (Meintjes, Leatt & Berry, 2005).

Further, in several households sampled, social assistance rather than paid employment was the main source of income. Results from the Census survey also supported a trend visible in the qualitative data, namely the strong imperative among adults, especially women, to seek work and contribute to household incomes.

As is the case in many impoverished communities in South and southern Africa, the rates of HIV prevalence are also very high, approximating one in five adults (Desmond Tutu HIV Centre, 2004; Thom, 2004). However, in contrast with many other areas at the time of the research, the roll-out of highly active antiretroviral therapy (a focus of two of the studies) was a reality in the communities and promised an alternative to prophylactic treatment and support groups for those with advanced disease.

Finally, two striking features of the ethnographic data are important for the discussion and can be clearly linked to the economic context described above. First, concerns around current or future scarcity are always present among residents (regardless of any possible effects of HIV) and the intensity of these changes with particular situational shifts, such as the gain or loss of employment (Bray & Brandt, 2005). Second, the everyday situations of parents and children can change rapidly and in various diverse ways, as individuals and domestic groups attempt to meet the needs of their members. Carers and children therefore often have to adjust to physical relocation, the arrival or departure of household members and changes in a carer's employment status and role in the home (ibid).

INCOME SHORTAGE AND THE IMPERATIVE TO SEEK WORK

Previous research on family life in poor urban Xhosa-speaking communities has drawn attention to the high level of adult mobility between these communities and rural areas of the Eastern Cape, much of which is driven by efforts to seek work. Understandably, an issue of concern in these studies is the possible effect of such movement on the care of children (Henderson, 1999; Jones, 1993; Spiegel & Mehlwana, 1997; Russell, 1995; Barbarin, Richter & De Wet, 2001). Opinions differ, but the dominant view is that mobility is problematic because it interferes with the continuity and consistency in care deemed necessary by psychologists for healthy development (for example Jones, 1993: 60, citing Rutter, 1976).

In light of research and the extent of movement evident in participants' life histories, we anticipated witnessing considerable mobility and changes in child-care arrangements. However, women carers on highly active antiretroviral therapy moved surprisingly little during the course of research. In the six-month fieldwork period, only one woman made a long journey to the Eastern Cape to visit her mother so that she could disclose her status to her. (Sadly, she died there.)

A closer look at women's weekly routines showed that HIV status, and particularly advanced-stage AIDS and treatment, can reduce mobility and associated interruptions in care relationships. Reasons to remain in one place include the regular appointments required by treatment regimens and the associated psychosocial inputs. All five women attended the clinic every one to four weeks (depending on their stage of treatment) for a medical check-up and adherence counselling, and four out of five of them had joined the weekly support group run by a local non-government organisation (NGO). In theory, this is a temporary scenario because people should in time be able to access similar supports from clinics elsewhere in the city and country, thereby limiting the constraints on mobility imposed by accessing highly active antiretroviral therapy. Such changes depend entirely on progress in antiretroviral roll-out, which has been slow thus far (Nattrass, 2006).

Despite the apparent advantages to the interpersonal and emotional dimensions to child care associated with continuity in relationships, there is a potential cost to reduced carer mobility in that work opportunities are restricted to those in their neighbourhood. Access to employment is further constrained by physical weakness and ill-health owing to advanced AIDS, associated infections (particularly tuberculosis) or, in a few cases, early adverse reactions to highly active antiretroviral therapy.

Some participants reported that ill health forced them to make choices that reduced or terminated their incomes (Brandt, in progress; Bray & Brandt, 2005). For example, one mother decided to open a *spaza* store in her own home thinking it would be a more manageable source of income than paid work for others (Bray & Brandt, 2005). Shortly after doing so, the symptoms of TB and HIV-related infections rendered her too sick to continue the business: "I was too weak to push the trolley of supplies from the supermarket to my home." Consequently, she became reliant on her partner's wage and social assistance in the form of the disability grant. Other mothers found ways of earning a small income, for example, by selling cigarettes and doing sewing jobs from home.

These findings point to the additional challenges to sick adults in poor communities posed by the range of work opportunities available, as well as the gendered nature of such opportunities. As Michael Bury (1982) has demonstrated in the context of chronic illness, the form of organisation of work tasks can reduce the strategies individuals have for masking or compensating for their illness or disabilities, and thereby offsetting the potential exacerbation of economic difficulties. Domestic work, waiting at tables in restaurants and office cleaning jobs are the most common sources of waged employment for women in the communities studied. All these involve a journey of at least half an hour, long hours on one's feet and both occupations often entail night work. More local options, such as babysitting or doing laundry for neighbouring families, also require reasonable health. Selling small amounts of groceries at minimal profit or hairdressing are about the only viable alternatives available to ill women. Local NGOs run small-scale income generation projects in the form of beading and sewing, but these are available to only a handful of women.

The situation for men is no easier and, in some ways, is more challenging owing to the physically demanding nature of the occupations available to unskilled or semi-skilled men. Gardening, construction and care-taking on business premises all require strength and good health. The fact that a large proportion of male employment is not regular waged work, but ad hoc daily employment acquired by standing on the side of the road, means that men are highly vulnerable to being without any income should their health fail. Men with some skills in car mechanics or electrical work are able to work from home, but these jobs also require physical fitness. Men are much less likely than women to engage in emerging employment in the social sector, for example HIV-related work such as peer education, adherence counselling or home-based care. Thus, while it remains the case that women are more likely to be infected with HIV, less likely to be employed and tend to have lower personal and household incomes (Brandt, 2006), the range of employment options available to them is greater than that available to men. Most importantly, however, the limited range of profitable home-based occupations available to poor unskilled people – both men and women – is clearly an obstacle to adults trying to provide adequate material care for children in the context of ill health.

An important feature of these findings, and one that is often sidelined in the literature, is that the ability to work and to provide materially for children is not predicted by HIV status per se, but by stage of illness. While women remain relatively well, and even where they have some degree of ill health, many nonetheless maintain their care-giving roles – including onerous jobs – at the expense of their own wellbeing.

Research elsewhere reports that HIV-positive women prioritise the needs of their children over their own (Bunting, 2001; Ciambrone, 2003; De Marco, Miller, Patsdaughter, Grindel & Chisholm, 1998; Mayers *et al.*, 2005) and are reluctant to admit practical difficulties imposed by their deteriorating health (Ciambrone, 2003). Our information does, however, point to one area where status seems to determine employment decisions. Some women chose to stop working even while relatively asymptomatic because of the difficulty of explaining intermittent periods of illness that occur during early-stage disease in the face of non-disclosure (Brandt, in progress). They reported fearing that they would lose their job once their status became known through their inability to perform at work. This scenario would entail the additional burden of people finding out about their status in a manner that they had no control over. A further important point is that severe health problems prompt difficulties in generating an income and caring for children, whether or not ill health arises from HIV.

Ironically, however, HIV – or more specifically the diagnosis of AIDS – can mean that there is less income shortage in the home. A household survey found HIV-affected households that reported regular income were more likely to be receiving state social assistance than households with unstable, irregular sources of income (ibid).

Of about one in five households not receiving state assistance that were able to generate regular income, none had an HIV-infected primary care-giver (ibid). The disability grant, which can be accessed by HIV-infected persons with either stage IV disease (a diagnosis of AIDS) or a CD4 count of less than 200, is one of the two most substantial grants, with the old-age pension[3], and a large proportion of people currently accessing the grant do so by virtue of their HIV status.

Thus, in the context of HIV, being sick can increase access to income, both through grants designed in part to respond to HIV-related needs (the disability grant, care dependency grant and foster care grant) and others for which household members are eligible (for example, the pension and child support grant), but who gain access through social worker assistance that followed the AIDS diagnosis. Consequently, grants play an important role in responding to immediate economic crises in households faced with poverty and HIV.

In terms of child care, regular income in the short term not only assists families in providing the material aspects of care, but stands to improve the psychosocial dimensions by reducing adult anxiety around the ability to provide (see section below on mental health). Reliance on grant income is, however, unstable in the long term because the disability grant can be terminated when there is a demonstrable improvement in health status, for example following highly active antiretroviral therapy treatment (Simchowitz, 2004).

The current structure of state social assistance means that there is no alternative grant accessible to people in this position (Whitworth, Wright & Noble, 2006). Thus, the flipside to the coin is that improvement in the health of HIV-positive adult carers might undermine the quality of child care owing to an abrupt loss of income and an associated increased anxiety for carers (see section on mental health below).

The degree to which grant loss affects child care is likely to depend partly on whether adult carers (and their household members or other providers) are able to sustain any employment during the treatment period and the value of their earnings.

We now turn to the effect of employment and HIV status on child care in spheres other than earning capacity and material provision. An interesting paradox arises from the dominant assumption that carer unemployment is problematic for poor children and that employment is optimal. Our data show some direct negative effects of carer unemployment (Bray & Brandt, 2005). For example, several mothers withdrew their children from crèche following the loss of their jobs because they could not afford the fees. However, in the context of the jobs available, employment entails carers spending large parts of the day, and even night, away from home and unavailable for child care. Some unemployed mothers of young children decided not to seek work in order to care for their children at home in the knowledge that their earnings would be minimal and not worth the trade-off against care for their children.

A history of communal care-giving can be protective in that neighbours and local kin perform many of the supervisory, instrumental and social care functions while parents are at work. The sharing of care responsibilities through such informal interaction is significant in that they might "serve as a buffer against the stresses of poverty, which in turn, may lead to more effective parenting practices" (Bromer & Henly, 2004: 944).

However, our data also point to some of the limitations of shared care-giving that emerge in consultation with children (Bray et al., in progress). One of the ingredients of good quality relationships and care identified by children aged nine years and upwards was spending time doing things with their parents or carers. They valued time together at home sharing everyday domestic tasks or relaxing in the evenings because these are the spaces in which intimate conversation occurs. And, despite being able to relax, eat and do homework with neighbours, children defined these aspects of care and the relationships that supported them as qualitatively different to their care relationships with parent figures, particularly with their "mothers" (ibid). We are careful to use the term parent figures here because many "fathers" are step-fathers and the "mothers" children speak about are often grandmothers or aunts who have nurtured them from a young age.

MENTAL HEALTH: A MEDIATOR TO QUALITY OF CARE

An additional factor in the relationship between adult employment and health status and their provision of child care is mental health. While various links between employment, HIV status and child care have been discussed, it is important to draw attention to the fact that mental health is often an overlooked mediator in the relationship between parental health and employment and child outcomes. Of course, this is largely a function of the fact that investigations of the effects of employment and health status tend to rely on household surveys and participant observation and therefore lack the psychological inquiry that draws attention to the role of mental health.

Parents and carers with whom we worked made a direct link between their own mental wellbeing and the quality of their interaction with, and care of, their children (Bray & Brandt, 2005):

> When I think of poor care...it's like when you push your children away when they are excited to show you something but your mind is consumed by worries about the next meal, or about a job or something like that.

> When small children receive care from a relaxed person it is clear how happy they look. My [HIV] status affects the energy I can give to my youngest child at the moment. She is left to do things for herself earlier than other children are. I cared for my older children in a more relaxed way when they were small [before I became infected]. I was not as pensive and worried.

Psychological testing and our observations of the interaction between mothers and their young children verify these mothers' own analyses of their poor mental state and its impact on effective care (ibid). For example, the mother in the second quotation cited above was suffering from symptoms of tuberculosis and was visibly weak physically, mentally and emotionally. At home, her responses to her lively five-year-old daughter were muted and discouraging of further engagement.

Interestingly, carers themselves recognise a relationship that is well-documented in the literature (ibid), namely that economic and social pressures, manifested particularly in the inability to provide materially for one's children, affects mental wellbeing and thus the emotional resources available to child care (Hundeide, 2002; Scheper-Hughes, 1992; Whiting & Edwards, 1989). Research has convincingly shown that poor psychological functioning in mothers, including depression, predicts poor monitoring of children and affects children's emotional and intellectual development (Cooper *et al.*, 1999; Forehand *et al.*, 2001; Jones *et al,*. 2002; Wild, 2001; see also Brandt, 2005b for a recent review).

Economic insecurities precipitated by unemployment clearly pose a risk to carers' mental health. Existing research suggests that the range of physical, mental and emotional stresses associated with being HIV-positive and AIDS sick can undermine mental health (see Brandt, 2005b). And, in the light of such high levels of co-incidence of unemployment and HIV, it is important to consider their combined effect on mental health. Research conducted in the United States, for example, found an association between high levels of depression and unemployment among HIV-infected women and mothers (Simoni *et al,*. 2000a; 2000b).

However, these relationships are not predictive. Rather, psychological research has identified other factors that moderate this relationship, including the social supports available to the individual carer and whether s/he has an internal or external locus of control (Klein *et al.*, 2000).[4] The presence of HIV (and decisions around disclosure) might heighten the influence of these factors, owing to changes in carer mental and functional health, as well as available social support (for more on this relationship, see Brandt, 2005a; Brandt, Dawes & Bray, 2006). Such dynamics illustrate the importance of social relationships in mediating mental wellbeing, while also serving to caution the researcher who may be trying to isolate linear causal relationships in generating an understanding of influences on child care.

SOCIAL SUPPORT AND SHARED CARE-GIVING

HIV can increase adults' need for support because of an inability to earn and because of poor physical and mental health. In this section we reflect on data showing sources of informal support used by adults in ensuring the care of their young children and question whether HIV status influences adults' considerations in their choices of support. We therefore address the question: what is the nature of social support where HIV-infected adults are faced with unemployment and thus often increased needs for both instrumental and emotional support? Our findings suggest that friends and neighbours might be providing a greater input to carers and thus to child care than is commonly recognised and that HIV is one factor in shaping this trend. We note also that choice of methods might influence our understanding of social networks, particularly in identifying differences between what people state to be their significant sources of support and those actually used.

Research has focused generally on the role of the extended family rather than friends or neighbours in providing support to carers and their children affected by HIV (and poverty and unemployment). A cursory look at the high degree of movement between Cape Town and the Eastern Cape would suggest that kin are the preferred sources of support. An analysis of women's social networks showed that only one-tenth rely heavily on extended family in the Eastern Cape and that the majority of support is provided by kin who live in the same household or neighbourhood (Brandt, in progress).

We found significant reliance on neighbourly friendships in certain communities (Bray & Brandt, in press at time of writing). Greater reliance on friends in the smaller and more recently settled townships seems to stem from the fact that fewer residents live with, or very close to, their extended families. These kin are often in the Eastern Cape or in larger townships some distance away. Residents of smaller communities are, therefore, more likely to have a history of shared care-giving for children in the immediate vicinity of their own home than with relatives.

The network analysis also showed gender to be a factor in that both men and women prefer to seek support from women (Brandt, in progress). For example, HIV-positive mothers drew primarily on close female relatives, particularly mothers, sisters and adult daughters.

Interestingly, however, a more nuanced perspective on support-seeking behaviour emerges from our qualitative and ethnographic material and serves to question if responses to questionnaires about one's social network provide sufficient insight into support-seeking behaviour. Both our observation of decision-making in the home and the in-depth interview transcripts show that HIV-positive adults have reasons to be worried about seeking support from family members and tend to cultivate or draw on relationships with friends and neighbours (Bray & Brandt, in press at time of writing). In some instances there is a direct link between HIV status and carers' decisions. In others, HIV is but one factor in a range of poverty-related pressures and constraints.

For carers who are HIV-positive, decisions on who to turn to for support are made in the context of how this would affect their wishes to disclose their HIV status or not, particularly in the case of family members. While disclosure can increase the level of support offered by family, it was evident in our conversations with HIV-infected and AIDS-sick mothers that they considered carefully if and how to disclose to certain family members in case it had negative effects on their relationship with that person (Brandt in progress, 2005a; Brandt, Dawes & Bray, 2006).

At our first interview with one mother, she had just disclosed to her brother, mother and boyfriend. By our second visit she had disclosed to her sister, who lives in a neighbouring shack. Her sister asked if she was HIV-positive because she had been seen frequenting the local clinic and support group, saying that she was also HIV-positive and had been scared to tell people. They had both been concealing their status from each other. The mother reports closer relationships within the extended family since making this discovery. They share food and space, meaning for example that the children eat in each other's homes, or in both when there is not enough to eat in one.

Interestingly, however, it is not only issues relating to disclosure that deter carers from seeking support from family at times of crisis, such as loss of employment (Bray & Brandt, in press at time of writing). One mother, who had disclosed her status to her kin in Cape Town, had entrusted her four-year-old son's care to two friends rather than her sister who lives two streets away. She explained this decision by recounting her previous experiences. Having moved in with her sister after losing a job, she described the shock and hurt that she and her son experienced when they were suddenly asked to leave on the grounds that they were becoming "too much for the household". She had anticipated a greater level of sympathy and generosity, especially given that she had disclosed her HIV status to her sister (who was an AIDS educator at the time). Following this experience, rather than moving in with, or near, her brother in another township, who has offered her consistent support over the years, she opted to find a new home for herself and her son, independently of family members.

The women carers described their considerations thus: On the one hand, they can reasonably expect a degree of support from close relatives. Ultimately, however, their decisions are outside their own sphere of control and there are high potential social and emotional costs to falling out of favour with their kin (Bray & Brandt, in press at time of writing). Reliance on neighbours and friends rather than kin might therefore have fewer complications and be more reliable.

MEN AND CHILD CARE
A further point that we believe deserves mention is the role of men in providing child care in the context of high levels of unemployment and HIV/AIDS. Previous research has painted a negative picture of male participation in family life. Some research pointed out the diminishing role of fathers in everyday care for children, arguing that, even for employed men, "the span of involvement within the household with their children and partners is shrinking" (Barbarin & Richter, 2001: 142). Others have suggested that connections between fathers and their children are

primarily, or evenly solely, articulated around material provision (Russell, 1995). In the light of typically pejorative representations of poor men and their role in child care within academic and popular spheres, we draw attention to findings that question these representations.

First, despite high rates of adult male mobility owing to employment constraints or relationship choices, children are often able to maintain connections with absent fathers through visits and cellphone conversations (Bray & Brandt, in press at time of writing). The sense of emotional connectedness children described with absent fathers was often strong, even in cases when physical contact had been sporadic. Recognition of the emotional dimension to care throws new light on an assumption that fathers who are physically absent (often because they are seeking employment elsewhere) do not contribute to child care.

Second, our data suggest that the normative discourse used by adults and children around material provision acts as a trope for care that includes important social and emotional dimensions (Bray & Brandt, in press at time of writing). When children first described or drew pictures of their fathers, they depicted them as sources of money and gifts. Only in later conversations and diary work was it apparent that children receive care from their fathers involving tenderness and nurture. It was clear that a certain level of trust and rapport with researchers was needed before children felt comfortable to recount actual experiences rather than social norms, thus highlighting the value of a long-term ethnographic approach.

Our observational data support the point that men living at home, and frequently unemployed, can and do play positive and supportive roles with respect to child care and the household more broadly (Bray & Brandt, in press at time of writing)[5]. Some of these contributions are indirect yet significant at both an emotional and material level, for example, the provision of residential security to mothers and young children through male ownership of plots and homes. Direct contributions included cooking, cleaning and playing with young children, the latter being particularly appreciated by mothers whose HIV-related mental and physical weakness made them unable to joke or play rough-and-tumble games.

In the light of prevailing norms, we were surprised by the degree of role flexibility between men and women that we observed in the home. Unemployed men – whether fathers, grandfathers or uncles – had more time available to perform these roles, but the fact that employed males were also active in the domestic and care realm in households with an HIV-positive carer indicated that practices might be shifting in response to the changes in the material, social and emotional environments of men and women.

Thus, in a context where male care is normatively regarded as requiring financial input, men who are both unemployed and absent from the home struggle to sustain both the material and emotional care roles. In practice, however, men are shown to be playing a more significant care role than is often assumed. Contrary to common assumptions, being an unemployed male does not equate with being a non-contributory father. The fact that these insights were derived from close observation in the home points to the value of ethnographic methods in understanding the flexibility of roles within the home in contexts of unemployment and ill-health.

CHILDREN'S CONTRIBUTIONS TO THEIR OWN AND OTHERS' CARE

In this final section we move beyond thinking about children as recipients of care and consider the manner in which they contribute to household production (and hence indirectly to their own care) in poor, HIV-affected communities and to the care of adults identified as their carers. Our findings suggest that new ways of conceptualising care are required if we are to account for the relationships between children and their carers made vulnerable through HIV, restricted employment opportunities and poverty.

As has been found in poor communities across the country, children begin doing domestic tasks from the age of five years, many of which directly assist their carers and thus contribute to the general care of all residents in the home (see Bray, 2003). These include helping with cooking, cleaning the home, washing their own and others' clothing and making tea for their carers. Many carry or watch over their younger siblings for periods of the day, or accompany them to and from crèche. Thus even young children perform roles that make it possible for adults to work outside the home. As age increases, so does engagement in activities that contribute directly to household incomes, for example selling goods from home or at the roadside. In a number of instances, teenagers fulfilled a vital role in facilitating adult carers' abilities to earn while juggling other domestic demands (Bray & Brandt, in press at time of writing). For example, one mother trained her 16-year-old daughter in hairdressing while she was pregnant so that her daughter could continue with customers while she attended to her baby. Such roles might prove to be more critical in the context of HIV/AIDS when adults are less able to work outside the home and sustain households economically.

While we had anticipated the extent and value of children's contributions to household production, we were surprised by their level of engagement in caring for their parents or adult care figures. Our data include striking examples of very young children who are actively involved in care, including the provision of emotional support (Bray & Brandt, in press at time of writing).

One four-year-old boy helped his mother with everyday domestic tasks, ensuring that she took her antiretroviral medication on time, inquiring about how she was feeling and giving her considerable emotional input. At the time no one else was living in their household and their relationship was clearly close and mutually supportive. These qualities had immediate emotional and social benefits for both and, for the son, included a sense of security in their small household unit. The mother's decision to disclose her status to her son seems to have contributed to a high level of trust between them. She now trusts him not to disclose her status to her own mother. The seriousness with which he approaches this and other responsibilities that come with his active engagement in caring for his mother indicates that he is proud of his role and derives considerable self-esteem from it.

Such active engagement in caring for an adult, and perhaps specifically a parent, appears to have considerable short-term benefits to children both directly (for example in enhanced self-esteem) and indirectly through supporting the carer's physical, mental and emotional wellbeing.[6] For example, the same mother said that her son's practical and emotional care boosts her own morale and gives her all the more reason to "live positively". Although unlikely to be consciously motivated, young children's efforts to look after and protect their carers bolster the mental health of these adults and thus (potentially) their capacity to care for their children. In this way children's active participation in caring for others can be effective in mitigating the effects of unemployment and ill-health on domestic relationships.

Finally, we draw attention to the implications of these findings for academic inquiry into care relationships involving children, particularly in the context of poverty, unemployment and HIV/AIDS. The first concerns the manner in which care is conceptualised and assessed in academic research. Children's efforts to care for their adult carers point clearly to the need to focus on relationships involving care rather than on only the care-giving activities by adults. The appropriateness of an approach to care that can encompass a two-way dynamic is further supported by our finding that older children value reciprocity highly in their relationships with both peers and adults (Bray & Gooskens, 2006).

Second, our findings pertaining to children's participation in care relationships point to an area for future research. The fact that some HIV-positive carers were not only reflecting openly on their children's attempts to understand and ameliorate their health-related vulnerabilities, but also on their own responses to such inputs from their children, suggest that HIV/AIDS might be opening up new ways of thinking about children's capacities and the possibilities within adult-child relationships. We suggest that this is a valuable avenue for research because if ways can be found to support carers in their recognition of the mutuality of care, they are arguably more likely to be making decisions that will enhance both their own wellbeing and that of their children. And in contexts when adult carers face the combined challenges of unemployment, poverty and HIV/AIDS, we envisage that they will experience the various ways in which children contribute to caring relationships as all the more valuable.

CONCLUSION

While many different approaches to the intersection of unemployment, HIV/AIDS and children are possible, we have restricted ourselves to conceptual issues that have emerged in our studies of children, women and child care in the contexts of poverty, unemployment and high HIV prevalence. Our analysis points clearly to the fallacy of the commonly assumed simple relationship between employment, HIV and child care, namely that HIV contributes to unemployment and income shortage, thereby directly and indirectly constraining and undermining the provision of adequate child care.

We have shown that adult carer employment has both costs and benefits to children, particularly when earnings are small. A research approach that prioritises children's views is able to draw out the emotional and social aspects of care that are performed in the day-to-day humdrum of shared domestic space. Children notice an impact on their care when work routines render adult carers physically unavailable, or when income and thus work-related anxiety renders them emotionally unavailable. The chapter also demonstrates the need to look beyond the material aspects of provision for children and the need to attend to the social and emotional resources available to them. And while HIV/AIDS has been shown to have certain specific influences on the availability of these resources (for example its effect on the mental health of carers), our findings clearly illustrate how important it is for researchers to study the broader social, economic and cultural context in which people living with HIV/AIDS are caring for children, including prevailing and pre-existing cultural practices.

A further conceptual point that emerges from our study concerns the extent to which research is able to capture and consider children's engagement in the processes under investigation. For example, our work on child care shows the limitations of studies that approach care as a one-way relationship of provision to children by adults. Once care is conceptualised as a relationship in which both parties give and receive, analysis of the particularities of these contributions and their effect on both adult and child wellbeing become possible. Such an approach allows us to identify the manner in which children's actions shape adult responses to different HIV and employment scenarios and thus their ability to provide care.

Precisely because HIV/AIDS, employment and child care are multi-dimensional experiences in that they involve physical, psychological and material resources, research that aims to understand the relationship between them needs to be equipped to document complexities and subtleties in cause and effect. To this end, we would strongly advocate a multi-disciplinary approach in future inquiry on these topics. The richness of the data generated in our research is largely attributable to a methodology that combined psychological and anthropological approaches. While the former provided insight into the mental health implications of HIV, employment and care, the latter were particularly helpful in documenting norms and ideals around the care relationship and contextualising these in observational data pertaining to everyday practice. Other disciplines stand to offer complimentary contributions. For example, a fine-grained economic analysis of the distribution of money and other material resources within households and domestic groups would provide different insights into relationships between employment, HIV/AIDS and children.

REFERENCES

Barbarin, O. & Richter, L. 2001. *Mandela's Children: Growing up in Post-Apartheid South Africa.* London: Routledge.

Barbarin, O., Richter, L. and de Wet, T. 2001. "Exposure to Violence, Coping Resources and Psychological Adjustment of Children," in *American Journal of Orthopsychiatry*, 71, 16 – 26.

Bauman, L. J., Camacho, S., Silver, E. J., Hudis, J., & Draimin, B. 2002. "Behavioral Problems in School-Aged Children of Mothers with HIV/AIDS," in *Clinical Child Psychology and Psychiatry*, 7, 39-54.

Brandt, R. (in progress). *Does HIV Matter When you are Poor and How? The Impact of*

HIV/AIDS in the Psychological Adjustment of Mothers in the era of HAART. Unpublished doctoral dissertation, Department of Psychology, University of Cape Town, Cape Town.

Brandt, R. 2006 *Does Mental Health Matter for Poor, HIV-infected Women/Mothers in the era of HAART?* CSSR Working Paper 06/139, University of Cape Town, Cape Town.

Brandt, R. 2005a. *Coping with HIV/AIDS: A Case Analysis of the Psychological Experiences of Poor, HIV-Positive Mothers and Women Caregivers in the era of HAART.* CSSR Working Paper 05/120, University of Cape Town, Cape Town.

Brandt, R. 2005b. *Maternal Wellbeing, Childcare and Child Adjustment in the Context of HIV/AIDS: What Does the Psychological Literature Say?* CSSR Working Paper 05/135, University of Cape Town, Cape Town.

Brandt, R., Dawes, A. & Bray, R. 2006. "Women Coping with AIDS in Africa: Contributions of a Contextually Grounded Research Methodology," in *Psychology, Health and Medicine,* 11(4), 522-527.

Bray, R. 2003. "Who Does the Housework? An Examination of South African Children's Working Roles," in *Social Dynamics,* 29, 95-131.

Bray, R. & I. Gooskens. 2006. "Ethics and the Everyday: Reconsidering Approaches to Research involving Children and Young People," in *Anthropology Southern Africa* 29 (1&2):35-44.

Bray, R. & Brandt, R. (in press at time of writing). "Childcare and Poverty in South Africa: An Ethnographic Challenge to Conventional Interpretations," in *The Journal of Children and Poverty.*

Bray, R. & Brandt, R. 2005 *What is Childcare Really About? An Ethnographic Analysis of Care Relationships in a Resource-poor Community.* CSSR Working paper 05/139, University of Cape Town, Cape Town. Available: http://www.cssr.uct.ac.za/pubs_csrr.html

Bray, R., Gooskens, I., Moses, S., & Seekings, J. (in progress) *Growing up in the New South Africa.* Book manuscript under preparation.

Bromer, J. & Henly, J. R. 2004. "Child Care as Family Support: Caregiving Practices across Child Care Providers" in *Children and Youth Services Review* 26 (10): 941-964.

Bunting, S. M. 2001. "Sustaining the Relationship: Women's Caregiving in the Context of HIV Disease," in *Health Care for Women International, 22,* 131-148.

Bury, M. 1982. "Chronic Illness as Biographical Disruption,"in *Sociology of Health and Illness,* 4 167-181.

Ciambrone, D. 2003 *Women's Experiences with HIV/AIDS: Mending Fractured Selves.* New York: The Haworth Press.

City of Cape Town, 2006. "City of Cape Town – Census 2001." Available: http://www.capetown.org.za/censusInfo/Census2001-new/Suburbs.htm

Cooper, P. J., Tomlinson, M., Swartz, L., Woolgar, M., Murray, L., & Molteno, C. 1999. "Post-Partum Depression and the Mother-Infant Relationship in a South African Peri-Urban Settlement," in *British Journal of Psychiatry,* 175, 554-558.

DeMarco, R., Lynch, M., & Board, R. 2002, "Mothers who Silence Themselves: A Concept with Clinical Implications for Women Living with HIV/AIDS and their Children," in *Journal of Pediatric Nursing,* 17, 89-95.

Denis, P. & Ntsimane, R. 2006. *The Absent Fathers: Why do Men not Feature in Stories of Families Affected by HIV/AIDS?,* in *Baba? Men and Fatherhood in South Africa,* ed by L. Richter and R. Morrell, 237-49. Cape Town: HSRC Press.

Desmond Tutu HIV Centre, 2004. Masiphumelele community survey. Unpublished data, Desmond Tutu HIV Centre, University of Cape Town, Cape Town.

Engle, P., Menon, P., Garrett, J. L., & Slack, A. 1997. "Urbanization and Caregiving: A Framework for Analysis and Examples from Southern and Eastern Africa," in *Environment and Urbanisation*, 9(2), 253-270.

Forehand, R., Armistead, L., Morse, E., Simon, P., & Clark, L. 2001. *The Family Health Project: An Investigation of Children whose Mothers are HIV-infected.* Available: www.apa.org/pi/aids/forehand.html

Giese, S., Meintjes, H., Croke, R., & Chamberlain, R. 2003. *Health and Social Services to Address the Needs of Orphans and other Vulnerable Children in the context of HIV/AIDS in South Africa: Research report and recommendations.* Report submitted to HIV/AIDS directorate, National Department of Health, January 2003. Cape Town: Children's Institute, University of Cape Town.

Gottlieb, A. 2004. *The Afterlife is Where We Come From: The Culture of Infancy in West Africa.* Chicago: The University of Chicago Press.

Henderson, P. 1999. *Living with fragility: Children in New Crossroads.* Unpublished Doctoral dissertation, Department of Social Anthropology, University of Cape Town.

Hundeide, K. 2002. *An outline of the ICDP Programme and its Theoretical Background.* Unpublished paper.

Jones, S. 1993. *Assaulting Childhood: Children's Experiences of Migrancy and Hostel Life in South Africa.* Johannesburg: Witwatersrand University Press.

Jones, D. J., Forehand, R., Brody, G., & Armistead, L. 2002. "Psychosocial Adjustment of African American Children in Single-Mother families: A Test of Three Risk Models," in *Journal of Marriage and Family,* 64 105-115.

Keigher, S., Zabler, B., Robinson, N., Fernandez, A., & Stevens, P. E. 2005. "Young Caregivers of Mothers with HIV: Need for Supports," in *Children and Youth Services Review,* 27, 881-904.

Klein, K., Armistead, L., Devine, D., Kotchick, B. A., Forehand, R., Morse, E. *et al.* 2000. "Socioemotional Support in African American Families Coping with Maternal HIV: An Examination of Mothers' and Children's Psychosocial Adjustment," in *Behavior Therapy,* 31, 1-26.

Leatt, A., Rosa, S. & Hall, K. 2005. " Towards a Means to Live: Targeting Poverty Alleviation to Realise Children's Rights,". in: Leatt, A. & Rosa, S. (eds.) *Towards a Means to Live: Targeting Poverty Alleviation to Make Children's Rights Real.* Cape Town: Children's Institute, University of Cape Town [CD-ROM].

Mann, G. 2001. *Networks of Support: A Literature Review of Care Issues for Separated Children.* Stockholm, Sweden: Save the Children.

Mann, G. 2002. *Family Matters: The Care and Protection of Children affected by HIV/AIDS in Malawi.* Stockholm, Sweden: Save the Children.

Mayers, A. M., Naples, N. A., & Nilsen, R. D. 2005. "Existential Issues and Coping: A Qualitative Study of Low-Income Women with HIV, in *Psychology & Health,* 20, 93-113.

Meintjes, H., Budlender, D., Giese, S., & Johnson, L. 2003. *Children 'in Need of Care' or in Need of Cash? Questioning Social Security Provisions for Orphans in the Context of the South African AIDS Pandemic.* Cape Town: Joint working paper of the Children's Institute and the Centre for Actuarial Research, University of Cape Town.

Meintjes, H., Leatt, A. & Berry, L. 2005. "Demography of South Africa's Children," in *South African Child Gauge 2005,* Jacobs, M., Shung-King, M. and C. Smith (eds). Cape Town: Children's Institute, University of Cape Town.

Montgomery, C., Hosegood, V., Busza, J. & I. Timaeus. 2006. "Men's Involvement in the South African Family: Engendering Change in the AIDS Era," in *Social Science and Medicine,* 62 (10): 2411-2419

Nattrass, N. 2006. *South Africa's 'Rollout' of Highly Active Antiretroviral Therapy: A Critical Assessment.* CSSR Working Paper No. 158, University of Cape Town, Cape Town. Available: http://www.cssr.uct.ac.za/pubs_cssr.html

Ramphele, M. 2002. *Steering by the Stars: Being Young in South Africa.* Cape Town: Tafelberg Publishers.

REPPSI. 2003. *Call to Action. Security and Stability: What Happens if we Neglect Children Affected by HIV/AIDS?* Southern African Development Commission Regional Consultative Meeting on Psychosocial Support Affected by HIV/AIDS, and the Security and Stability Implications of HIV/AIDS for the SADC Region.

Reynolds, P. 1989. *Children in Crossroads: Cognition and Society in South Africa.* Cape Town: David Phillip.

Reynolds, P. 1995. *The Ground of all Making: State Violence, the Family and Political Activists.* HSRC report HG/MF-24.

Richter, L., Manegold, J., & Pather, R. 2004. *Family and Community Interventions for Children Affected by AIDS.* Cape Town: HSRC Publishers.

Russell, M. 1995. *Parenthood Among Black Migrant Workers to the Western Cape: Migrant Labour and the Nature of Domestic Groups.* Co-operative research programme on marriage and family life. HSRC report HG / MF – 22.

Rutter, M. 1976. "Parent-Child Separation: Psychological Effects on the Children," in A. Clarke and A. Clarke (eds.), *Early Experience: Myth and Evidence.* London: Open Books.

Scheper-Hughes, N. 1992. *Death Without Weeping: The Violence of Everyday Living in Brazil.* Berkeley: University of California Press.

Shonkoff, J. P. & Meisels, S. J. 2000. *Handbook of Early Childhood Intervention* (2nd ed.) Cambridge: Cambridge University Press.

Simchowitz, B. 2004. *Social Security and HIV/AIDS: Assessing "Disability" in the Context of ARV Treatment.* CSSR Working Paper No. 99, University of Cape Town, Cape Town. Available: http://www.cssr.uct.ac.za/pubs_cssr.html

Simoni, J., Demas, P., Mason, H., Drossman, J. A., & Davis, M. L. 2000a. "HIV Disclosure Among Women of African Descent: Association with Coping, Social Support and Psychological Adoption," in *AIDS and Behavior,* 2, 147-158.

Simoni, J. M., Davis, M. L., Drossman, J. A., & Weinberg, B. A. 2000b. "Mothers with HIV/AIDS and their Children: Disclosure and Guardianship Issues," in *Women & Health,* 30, 39.

Snider, L. 2003. *Indicators for Psychosocial Programs.* Paper presented at the OVC Technical Consultation, Washington, DC, November 3-5.

Spiegel, A. & Mehlwana, A. 1997. *Family as Social Network: Kinship and Sporadic Migrancy in the Western Cape's Khayelitsha.* Co-operative research programme in marriage and family life. HSRC report HG / MF – 31.

Swartz, L., Brandt, R., Dawes, A., Bray, R., Mthembu-Salter, L., & Tomlinson, M. 2005. *An Exploratory Study of the Impact of Primary Caregiver HIV Infection on Caregiving and Child Developmental Outcome in the Era of HAART* – Report for the Organization for Social Science Research in Eastern and Southern Africa (OSSREA): HIV/AIDS Challenge for Africa Research Programme. Cape Town: HSRC and University of Cape Town.

Thom, A. 2004. W. Cape Plots HIV Rates by District. Available: http://csa.org.za/article/articlereview/326/1/1/

Tolfree, D. K. 2003. *Community Based Care for Separated Children.* Save the Children: Sweden.

UNAIDS/UNICEF 2004. *A Framework for the Protection, Care and Support of Orphans and Vulnerable Children Living in a World with HIV and AIDS.* Report prepared for the Global Partners Fund, May.

Whiting, B. & C. Edwards. 1989. *Children of Different Worlds.* Cambridge: Harvard University Press.

Whitworth, A., Wright, G., & Noble, M. 2006. *A Review of Income Transfers to Disabled and Long Term Sick People in Seven Case Study Countries and Implications for South Africa.* Working Paper no. 5, Centre for the Analysis of South African Social Policy, Department of Social Policy and Social Work, University of Oxford.

Wild, L. 2001. "Review: The Psychosocial Adjustment of Children Orphaned by AIDS," in *Southern African Journal of Child and Adolescent Mental Health,* 13, 3-22.

Young, L. & Ansell, N. 2003. "Fluid Households, Complex Families: The Impacts of Children's Migration as a Response to HIV/AIDS in Southern Africa," in *The Professional Geographer,* 55 (4). 464-476.

---

[1] More recent work by UNICEF (2005) that is also part of an ongoing project to inform national monitoring and evaluation (M&E) strategies with respect to orphans and children made vulnerable by HIV/AIDS, looks more comprehensively at psychosocial wellbeing, including the strengthening of families' capacities for care for these children. Whether, and to what extent, the nature of care relationships is considered in this approach remains to be seen when more detailed monitoring strategies are published.

[2] The interested reader is referred to the following papers and reports: Brandt (in progress; 2005a); Brandt, Dawes and Bray (2006); Bray and Brandt (in press at time of writing); Bray (2003); Bray and Gooskens (2006); Bray, Gooskens, Moses and Seekings (in progress); and Swartz, Brandt, Dawes, Bray, Mthembu-Salter and Tomlinson (2005).

[3] At the time of data collection, both the pension and disability grants were equal to R780, while the foster care grant was R540 and the Care Dependency Grant and Child Support Grants R180 per month.

[4] This term, as used by psychologists in particular, refers to the extent to which someone perceives events in their external environment to be within their control. Someone with an external locus of control tends to perceive herself as having little control over her environment, while someone with an internal locus of control refers to someone who perceives herself as having agency in relation to the events in her life.

[5] For recent examples of roles played by men in the context of HIV/AIDS, see Denis and Ntsimane (2006) and Montgomery et al. (2006).

[6] Elsewhere we have also discussed the potentially adverse longer-term consequences for children of adopting parental roles (see Keigher et al., 2005). However, it must also be mentioned that children's participation in forms of care and other household activities is a norm in many poor communities and that this should be considered when evaluating the impact on child outcomes in the context of HIV/AIDS.

CHAPTER 7

REALISING CHILDREN'S RIGHTS THROUGH SOCIAL SERVICES:
DETERMINING THE DEPARTMENT OF SOCIAL DEVELOPMENT'S INITIATIVES

MARIO CLAASEN

INTRODUCTION

The apartheid legacy has left millions of children and their families vulnerable. The new government of 1994 had the onerous task of rectifying the imbalances between South Africa's children. The government introduced several pro-poor policies to transform the social sector (health, education and social development) that would ultimately reap long-term benefits for the poor.

One of the social sector departments that directly fights poverty is the Department of Social Development. The primary poverty-alleviation programme is the department's social assistance programme, which provides cash grants directly to beneficiaries, including children. Another poverty-related programme is the social welfare services that the department, with non-governmental organisations, delivers to the poor and vulnerable. These services include crime prevention or diversion programmes, alternative care, home- and community-based HIV/AIDS care, etc. These two programmes are interrelated, but often the functions are fragmented at provincial or district level. This affects the department's obligations to fulfil the rights of children.

This chapter examines what the government's obligations are to children living in poverty, how the government fulfils these obligations and how it deals with the challenges that face the social assistance and social welfare programmes. The chapter provides an overview of the situation of children living in poverty. It examines the statutory obligations of the South African government in terms of the Constitution and other legal frameworks. It reviews the role of the Department of Social Development at a national and provincial level, as well as transformation developments in social assistance, focusing on social welfare services. The budget for both social assistance and social welfare programmes is analysed.

CHILDREN IN CONTEXT

In 2004, South Africa had just more than 18 million children. Children made up 49% of the South African population. At provincial level KwaZulu-Natal had the highest number of children (21%), followed by the Eastern Cape (18%), Gauteng (15%) and Limpopo (14%). By population group, black children were in the majority at 84%, while coloured children made up 8% of the population. The gender breakdown of all children was almost equal between girls and boys (www.childrencount.ci.org.za).

An important indicator related to children is income poverty. Income helps children to get their basic needs met. If there is a lack of income in the household, this will affect children's wellbeing. In 2004, the percentage of children living in income poverty was 66%. In absolute terms this means that 11.9 million children were living in households with an income of R1 200 a month or less. The child poverty rate differed across provinces. Limpopo had the highest rate of child poverty at 81%. The Eastern Cape (79%), Mpumalanga (70%), KwaZulu-Natal (69%) and the Free State (68%) had a higher child poverty rate than the national average (ibid).

Poverty is closely linked to the standard of living and this affects children's wellbeing in a range of ways. HIV and AIDS are among the conditions that affect one's standard of living. In 2000 it was estimated that 40% of deaths of children under the age of five were due to AIDS.

Related to this is orphanhood. In 2004, there were about 3.3 million orphans in South Africa. Orphans are defined as children who have lost a biological mother, father or both parents. In 2004, 25% of orphans were living in KwaZulu-Natal and 22% were living in the Eastern Cape (ibid). These provinces also had a high prevalence of HIV/AIDS.

The kind of dwelling in which children live can also be problematic. Almost two million children live in inadequate housing, ie backyard dwellings or shacks in informal settlements. Informal settlements are notorious for being hazardous to those living there because of risks such as shack fires and paraffin poisoning (ibid). In informal settlements there also are problems getting clean water and adequate sanitation. In 2004, 43% of children lived in households with inadequate water. In the Eastern Cape more than 76% of children had an inadequate supply of water, whereas in Gauteng and the Western Cape only 8 % and 7% of children had an inadequate water supply respectively (ibid).

In 2004, 49% of children did not have adequate sanitation. Adequate sanitation is vital to maintain good hygiene and avoid exposure to worms and bacterial infection. The Eastern Cape had the highest rate for inadequate sanitation amongst children in 2004 with 73%; this was followed by Limpopo with 71% (ibid).

Millions of children live in poverty and in other deplorable conditions. The key response from the government to children living in poverty is social assistance, delivered by the Department of Social Development. In addition to this service, the department is also responsible for social welfare services that aim to lessen the causes of poverty. This forms part of the state's obligations to those living in poor conditions, including children.

THE STATE'S OBLIGATIONS TO CHILDREN

All states have obligations to their citizens. These obligations are declared in national constitutions and in regional and international treaties. Government parties and non-government parties must *respect, protect* and *fulfil* the rights of citizens, who give the state their mandate through the electoral process. To fulfil its obligations to its citizens, the state has to develop policies or legal frameworks and programmes and budget for each programme. Since socioeconomic rights are realised over time, the government's programmes must not be regressive either in terms of service delivery or budget allocation. This forms the foundation of the obligations the state has to its citizens.

The South African Constitution (1996) is the national framework for the state's obligations to its citizens. In particular, Chapter Two, the Bill of Rights, outlines the political, civil, social, economic and cultural rights of everyone in the country. The socioeconomic rights enshrined in the Bill of Rights include the rights to housing, health care, food, water, social security and basic and further education. There are also child-specific rights under section 28. Section 281(c) affords children four socioeconomic rights: basic nutrition, shelter, basic health care services and social services. Children are also entitled to adequate housing (section 26(1)) and to basic education (section 29 (1)(a)). The socioeconomic rights stated in the Constitution are just, ie these rights can be brought within the legal framework and presented before the courts, leading to a measure of enforcement or provision of remedies (Streak & Wehner, 2004b: 54).

There is a distinction between the rights stated in section 26 and 27 and those afforded to children in section 28 (1)(c) and 29 (1)(a). The former rights are limited by provision 27(2) which states that: "The state must take reasonable legislative and other measures, within its available resources, to achieve the progressive realisation of each of these rights". The child-specific rights, on the other hand, place no limitations on the state's delivery obligations. This has resulted in debates about whether the child-specific rights are basic rights and should be delivered at the basic level or not (ibid). These debates continue.

Related to this issue is the question of what should be delivered. The Constitution does not detail the content or range of the socioeconomic rights the state should deliver. This means that the state, in meeting its obligations towards children and others, can subjectively decide what level of services to deliver (ibid: 54).

The Constitutional Court was reluctant to lay down a minimum core of basic entitlements. The *Grootboom* (*Government of the Republic of South Africa and Others v Grootboom and Others (1) SA 46 (CC)*) case was the first time the Constitutional Court tried to determine the government's realisation of socioeconomic rights. The case focused on the right of access to adequate housing. The Court admitted that the Constitution does not stipulate any measure to government on socioeconomic rights. To remedy this, the Court provided direction on how the state should meet its measures. This was done by the "reasonable measures test" that the Court used to assess if the state's programmes for section 26 rights complied with its constitutional requirements.

The Court applied this test again in the *Treatment Action Campaign* case in 2002 (ibid: 64; Rosa & Dutschke, 2006: 19). The requirements for a government programme to meet its constitutional obligations of the measures test are as follows (Streak & Wehner, 2004b: 65):

• The programme is reasonable both in its inception and in its implementation;
• The programme is balanced and flexible;
• It makes appropriate provision for crises and gives attention to short-, medium- and long-term needs;
• The programme does not exclude a significant segment of society; and
• The programme takes into account the degree and extent of the denial of the right it is trying to realise. It does not ignore those whose needs are most urgent.

The above criteria have become the measure for the judiciary by which most of the government's programmes are assessed for meeting their constitutional obligations to the realisation of socioeconomic rights.

Government parties' obligations to citizens are also laid out in regional and international treaties. South Africa has ratified two key treaties related to children's socio-economic rights and, by doing so, has entered into a legal agreement to meet the rights set out in the treaties. The two treaties are the African Charter on the Rights and Welfare of the Child (ACRWC) and the Convention on the Rights of the Child (CRC). Both treaties afford children a comprehensive set of political, civil, social, economic and cultural rights.

Article 4 of the CRC says states are obliged to take "all appropriate legislative, administrative and other measures for the implementation of the rights" of children (CRC, 1989; Streak & Wehner, 2004b: 56). The rights included in the CRC are the right to a full and decent life for disabled children (Article 23); the right to the highest attainable standard of health (Article 24); the right to social security (Article 26); the right to basic education (Article 28) and the right to be protected from exploitation and hazardous working conditions (Article 32) (CRC, 1989).

The ACRWC was developed by the Organisation of African Unity (OAU) in 1990 and was ratified by South Africa in January 2000. It affords similar rights to children as set out in the CRC: the right to education (Article 11); rights of disabled children (Article 13); the right to the best attainable health care and health services (Article 14) and protection from exploitative labour practices (Article 15) (ACRWC, 1990). Unlike the CRC, the ACRWC makes no mention of a child's right to social assistance. However, Article 20 (2) says states should help parents with material assistance and programmes. This article can be considered to include social assistance provision (ACRWC, 1990; Streak & Wehner, 2004: 57).

Both treaties recognise that responsibility for children lies with both parents, but also makes provision for state help when the parents do not have the means to provide for the needs of the child. This provision was recognised in the *Grootboom* case in the High Court, but was rejected by the Constitutional Court on the grounds that the Court made a distinction between children with and without family support and within the family environment (Rosa & Dutschke, 2006: 19).

Although international treaties legally require government parties to implement the provisions set out, they are difficult to enforce. Government parties that ratify the CRC must report every five years on the implementation of the CRC to the Committee on the Rights of the Child. Non-government parties can also present "shadow" reports to the committee. This allows non-government parties to report their perspective of their country's implementation of the CRC, which might differ from the government's perspective. Often this is the only means at international level to monitor the progress of the implementation of a treaty. However, enforcement of the treaty is still weak.

The South African Constitution has more weight in terms of enforcing a child's right because it is the supreme law of the country. This is an important tool to hold government accountable in terms of its obligations to children and their wellbeing. The government has made several strides in ensuring the rights and wellbeing of children and one of the key departments implementing its obligations to children is the Department of Social Development.

CHILD-SPECIFIC GOVERNMENT PROGRAMMES

To realise the rights stated in the Constitution, government has to develop policies or legal frameworks that give effect to these rights. But these policies need to be translated into programmes to ensure implementation. Often programmes are conceptualised by national departments and implemented by provincial departments. The national departments allocate funds to the provincial departments to deliver the programmes. The funds are allocated either as an equitable share (ie general provincial funds to be used at its discretion) or in the form of conditional grants (ie grants with certain conditions attached on what and how the funds should be spent). Table 1 outlines some of the child-specific government programmes delivered at provincial level and their child-related socioeconomic rights.

TABLE 1: CHILD-SPECIFIC PROGRAMMES IMPLEMENTED BY PROVINCIAL GOVERNMENTS

CHILD SOCIOECONOMIC RIGHT	PROGRAMME TITLE	SERVICE PROGRAMME AIMS TO PROVIDE	TARGETED BENEFICIARIES
SOCIAL DEVELOPMENT DEPARTMENT PROGRAMMES			
Right to social services	Child Support Grant (CSG)	Monthly payment of R190 (from 1 April 2006), claimed by the caregiver on behalf of the child.	Targeted at children aged 0-14 who pass a means test.
Right to social services	Care Dependency Grant (CDG)	Monthly payment of R820 (from 1 April 2006) claimed by the caregiver on behalf of the child.	Targeted at poor children who have severe mental or physical disabilities and are in need of full-time care.
Right to social services and right to alternative care	Foster Care Grant (FCG)	Monthly payment of R590 (from 1 April 2006) claimed by the caregiver with a court order indicating their foster care status.	Targeted at children who are placed in foster care by a social worker on behalf of the children's court.
Right to alternative care and right to protection	Secure Care Programme	Provides shelter for children who have been removed from their homes.	Targeted at neglected, abused and/or exploited children.
Right to alternative care and right to protection	Transformation of the Child and Youth Care Programme	Provides transformation homes, places of safety, as well as quality assurances from these places that the programmes are being implemented and are working.	This programme targets children in conflict with the law and children in need of protection.
EDUCATION DEPARTMENT PROGRAMMES			
Right to nutrition	Primary school feeding scheme	Early morning nutritious supplementary meal.	Targets primary school learners from poor households. Schools with the highest levels of poverty, rural schools, farm schools and informal schools are targeted.
Right to education	Public Ordinary Schooling	Provision of ordinary schooling to all learners from the compulsory schooling band (1-9) and older (grade 10-12).	Targeted at children who need compulsory schooling (grade 1-9) and wanting further education and training (grade 10-12).
HEALTH DEPARTMENT PROGRAMMES			
Right to basic health care	Free health care for children	Aims to provide all health services provided by state health facilities, with emphasis on the primary level of care free.	Children under six years and pregnant women who are not covered by a medical scheme and using public sector facilities are targeted.

Adapted from Streak, J, 2004a, Government spending on children in MTEF 2004/05: Spotlighting social development programmes, Budget Information Service, IDASA

All of the above programmes in the three social sector departments play a vital role in advancing children's rights. The Department of Social Development's role however, specifically focuses on human development and on improving the lives of the poor and vulnerable in society. This chapter focuses on the department's efforts to eradicate child poverty and its root causes.

THE ROLE AND FUNCTION OF THE NATIONAL AND PROVINCIAL DEPARTMENTS OF SOCIAL DEVELOPMENT

The vision and mission of the social development departments are to have an integrated system of social development services that facilitate human development and improve the quality of life of the poor and vulnerable in society. The departments deliver on their mandate through various functions. The national department's and the provincial departments' functions differ. The national department's functions include (www.welfare.gov.za):

• The development of policies and legislation to achieve its strategic objectives;
• The development of strategies and programmes that give effect to the department's policies and legislation;
• The development of norms and standards for the delivery of services;
• Providing support to provincial departments, non-governmental organisations (NGOs) and community-based organisations (CBOs) in the implementation of strategies and programmes;
• Monitoring and evaluating the effect of policies and programmes and the expenditure of conditional grants to the provincial departments;
• Conducting research on social development issues. Advising the minister on a range of budgetary matters related to the social development sector; and
• Communicating and disseminating information on the social development sector.

The provincial departments deliver the services, but they also contract several NGOs and CBOs to deliver services directly to clients. Some of these include (ibid):

• Payment of relief to victims of declared disasters;
• Registration of non-profit organisations;
• Payment of social grants to those eligible;
• Payment of subsidies to national councils;
• Poverty-relief projects; and
• Home-based/community-based HIV/AIDS projects.

There are key policies and legislation which govern the Department of Social Development's functions (Department of Social Development, 2006):

• Social Assistance Act, 1992 (Act No 59 of 1992);
• South African Social Security Agency Act, 2004 (Act No 9 of 2004);
• Non-Profit Organisations Act, 1997 (Act No 71 of 1997);
• Probation Services Act, 1991 (Act No 116 of 1991);
• Child Care Act, 1983 (Act No 74 of 1983);
• Aged Persons Act, 1967 (Act No 81 of 1967);
• National Development Agency Act, 1998 (Act No 108 of 1998);
• White Paper for Social Welfare (1997);
• White Paper on Population Policy for South Africa (1998);
• Service Delivery Model for Developmental Social Services (2006).

From 1 April 2006 social assistance delivery became a national function, with the establishment of the South African Social Security Agency (Sassa). The provincial departments' core programme functions are social welfare services and development and research.

This transformation was welcomed because social welfare services have been neglected since the advent of democracy in South Africa. Social welfare services play an important role in poverty alleviation because programmes aim to provide the poor and vulnerable with the capacities, tools and resources necessary to resolve their problems independently. It is envisioned that welfare services will have a new approach, based on the following (Streak & Poggenpoel, 2005c: 17-18):

- A developmental focus and service method;
- Emphasis on prevention and early intervention strategies;
- Fewer services located at the continuum of care level, but well-resourced and highly effective;
- Integrated services, including special developmental areas;
- Services that form links with and integrate social assistance sections;
- Services with a strong focus on anti-poverty strategies; and
- Services addressing the needs of children, youth and families and/or woman and older persons.

TRANSFORMATION OF SOCIAL WELFARE SERVICES

The focus for more than a decade in the social welfare sector has been on social security provision. This has "crowded out" resources for other essential services like social welfare services and has had a negative effect on the social welfare sector's ability to deliver social welfare services (Social Development, 2006):

- Protection services have been inadequately developed;
- There are not enough social service practitioners to deal with the increasing case-load and poverty;
- There is a great number of children who have to wait in prison before being tried because of an inadequate number of probation officers and lack of infrastructure, such as places of safety and secure care facilities in communities;
- Planning is hampered by the lack of an information management system;
- There are inadequate prevention and early intervention services;
- There has been a loss of skilled personnel because of low salaries and difficult working conditions;
- There have been increased social pathologies, such as the number of street children, the number of orphaned children due to HIV/AIDS, etc; and
- There has been a collapse of services or services have been reverted to the state because of the lack of adequate resources given to the NGO sector to render these services.

To adequately respond to this the national Department of Social Development developed the Service Delivery Model for Developmental Social Welfare Services. This model aims to provide a framework allowing social welfare services to adopt a developmental approach to the nature, scope, extent and level of its services. The developmental approach places a high value on the role of the client, who is an active recipient and participant in the delivery of social welfare services. This approach differs in the way it views the client and in how it addresses the problems that lead to social pathologies.

On a programmatic level it also aims to integrate the three social development services: social security, social welfare and development and support services. The three have been largely fragmented and difficult to coordinate at a provincial level. However, the shift of social security provision to the national sphere frees up essential resources – both human and financial – that can be dedicated to social welfare services.

FUNDING FOR SOCIAL DEVELOPMENT SERVICES –
2001/02 TO 2005/06

SOCIAL ASSISTANCE PROVISION

Since 1998 provincial governments have delivered three child-related social assistance programmes: the child support grant (CSG), the foster care grant (FCG) and the care dependency grant (CDG). The CSG is targeted specifically at children living in poverty, while the FCG aims to assist children who are in need of care. The CDG is intended to provide support for care-givers who have children, between the ages of one and 18 years, with physical and mental disabilities. To date there is no government clarity on how chronically ill children with HIV/AIDS can access the CDG (Streak, 2005d: 3).

The different grants are also for different amounts; from 1 April 2006 the CSG stood at R190 a month, the FCG at R590 and the CDG at R820. Children who are under the age of 14 years are eligible for the CSG. The primary care-giver also has to pass a means test, which states the following criteria: the care-giver and child must live in an urban area in a formal dwelling and personal income must be below R9 600 a year; or in a rural area in a formal or informal dwelling with a personal income of below R13 200 a year. Although the amount of the CSG and other grants has increased with inflation since its implementation, the means test has not been adjusted for inflation since 1998 (Streak, 2005d: 2). From March 2006 just over seven million children were beneficiaries of the CSG (Leatt, 2006: 7). The number of children eligible for the CSG, at a national level, using a means test adjusted for inflation, is estimated to be 9 308 547 between the ages of 0-14. Using a means test not adjusted for inflation, it was found that 8 791 705 children aged 0-14 are eligible for the CSG (Streak, 2005d: 6; Leatt, 2006: 10).

The FCG is intended to be an incentive for non-biological care-givers to foster children who are in need of care. The means test for the FCG does not take into consideration the income of the foster parents, but it does consider the child's income which should not exceed twice the annual amount of the FCG. The FCG is not intended as a poverty-relief grant, but this has been the case because thousands of care-givers have taken in children who have been orphaned because of AIDS and they receive the grant to meet the child's basic needs. This has created an increased demand for the FCG and there has not been an increase in the number of social workers and magistrates at children's courts to deal with this increased demand and case load (Streak, 2005d: 3; Leatt, 2006: 4).

There are some gaps in the grant system related to children's needs (Streak, 2005d: 4):

- Children who suffer from chronic illnesses (like HIV/AIDS-related infections and asthma) do not qualify for any form of income support to cater for their special needs;
- Children aged 15-18 years and their care-givers who qualify according to the means test cannot access the CSG;
- The means test for the CSG has not been adjusted for inflation since the programme's inception; and
- The use of the FCG as a poverty-relief grant is draining resources and could cripple the child-care protection system.

Even with these gaps, the social assistance programme reaches more than ten million children in need (Leatt, 2006). An assessment of the effect of the grants on children's wellbeing is not yet known, but the programme is a most effective and immediate short-term poverty-alleviation programme targeting child poverty. However, for this programme to be optimally efficient and effective, it is dependent on social welfare services for ensuring the sustainable development of individuals (children and youth) and communities to develop their full potential to become active agents of their own lives.

PROVINCIAL SOCIAL WELFARE SERVICES

At provincial level social welfare services comprise two programmes: the social welfare services programme and the development and support services programme. The social welfare programme comprises the following sub-programmes:

- Treatment and prevention of substance abuse;
- Care of older persons;
- Crime prevention and support;
- Services to people with disabilities; and
- Child and family care and protection services.

The development and support services programme's sub-programmes differ slightly across provinces, but three sub-programmes are present across provinces:

- Youth development;
- HIV/AIDS; and
- Poverty alleviation.

The social welfare services programme and the development and support services programme are combined in the budget analysis and are compared with the social assistance programme.

SPENDING AND ALLOCATIONS TO SOCIAL ASSISTANCE AND SOCIAL WELFARE SERVICES

The budget analysis of funds was compiled using data from the 2005/06 provincial statements. The data for 2001/02, 2002/03 and 2003/04 represent amounts that have been audited. The data for 2004/05 are revised estimates, while 2005/06 – 2007/08 represent data over the medium-term expenditure framework (MTEF). The 2005/06 provincial statements were chosen because the 2006/07 provincial statements do not include social assistance data, making it difficult to compare the social assistance programme with the social welfare programme. The social welfare programme comprises data from both the social welfare and developmental and support services programmes of provinces. The 2005/06 provincial statements for Limpopo were not available at the time of writing and so are not included.

Table 2 indicates the share of resources spent (2001/02 – 2004/05) and budget allocations (2005/6 – 2007/08) on social assistance and social welfare as a proportion of provincial expenditure and budget allocations.

Table 2 indicates the following trends. First, the proportion of provincial budgets spent on social welfare between 2001/02 – 2004/05 signifies a small proportion, while social assistance spending is significantly higher across all provinces. Second, there is a slight increase of welfare spending between 2001/02 – 2004/05 in provinces, but this increase still remains a small proportion of provincial spending. The increase for all provinces is from 1.64% in 2001/02 to 3.29% by 2004/05, with a declining trend over the MTEF period. Third, there are variations in the proportion spent on social welfare among provinces. In 2004/05, for instance, Free State (2.02%), the Eastern Cape (4.22%) and Western Cape (2.24%) have larger proportions compared to KwaZulu-Natal (1.14%), North-West (1.33%) and Mpumalanga (1.28%). Last, the proportion for spending projected over the MTEF is small or stagnant across all provinces. This indicates that social welfare is less of a priority across provinces. Even the National Treasury admitted that the social assistance programme was crowding out resources from the social welfare programme (National Treasury, 2006: 49).

This is quite worrying because the Department of Social Development's Service Delivery Model for Developmental Social Services places a higher priority on social welfare services, but this is not matched by budget allocations over the MTEF period.

TABLE 2: SOCIAL ASSISTANCE AND SOCIAL WELFARE PROPORTION OF PROVINCIAL SPENDING

PROGRAMME 2: SOCIAL ASSISTANCE	2001/02	2002/03	2003/04	2004/05	2005/06 MTEF	2006/07 MTEF	2007/08 MTEF
Gauteng	12.13	13.80	16.40	17.97	20.37	20.63	20.72
Free State	15.98	19.49	22.11	24.47	27.22	27.66	27.80
Eastern Cape	22.23	24.45	26.82	29.91	31.18	31.32	30.82
KwaZulu-Natal	18.70	22.39	25.38	28.00	28.02	27.65	27.27
Mpumalanga	16.67	19.05	21.58	23.03	25.06	25.55	24.67
North-West	18.39	20.86	23.81	25.35	26.44	27.07	27.32
Northern Cape	21.23	23.25	24.59	24.59	26.39	25.94	26.04
Western Cape	14.98	18.52	19.31	19.99	20.50	20.11	20.66
ALL PROVINCES	**17.54**	**20.23**	**22.50**	**24.22**	**25.65**	**25.74**	**25.66**
PROGRAMME 3: SOCIAL WELFARE							
Gauteng	2.31	2.04	1.64	1.88	1.45	1.45	1.33
Free State	1.64	1.60	1.90	2.02	2.03	2.08	1.98
Eastern Cape	1.16	1.06	1.24	4.22	1.25	1.27	1.26
KwaZulu-Natal	1.05	1.00	1.11	1.14	1.47	1.44	1.39
Mpumalanga	0.87	1.22	1.11	1.28	1.19	2.08	1.88
North-West	1.30	1.45	1.68	1.33	1.40	1.48	1.51
Northern Cape	2.34	2.12	1.90	2.02	2.33	2.24	2.25
Western Cape	2.41	2.28	2.23	2.24	2.35	2.19	2.10
ALL PROVINCES	**1.64**	**1.60**	**1.60**	**3.29**	**1.68**	**1.78**	**1.71**

Source: Provincial Budget Statements 2005/06 and own calculations.

Table 3 provides an overview of the proportions of the social assistance and social welfare programmes. At first glance, one notices the large proportion of provincial social development spending and projected budgets over the MTEF are dedicated to the social assistance programme. Between 2001/02 and 2004/05 there is, across all provinces, a declining trend of the share of social development budgets being spent on social welfare services and this trend continues over the MTEF. The allocation given to social welfare services again is not adequate. This has severe consequences for the essential services that are there to protect children from all forms of harm and abuse.

TABLE 3: SOCIAL ASSISTANCE AND SOCIAL WELFARE PROPORTION OF SOCIAL DEVELOPMENT BUDGETS

PROGRAMME 2: SOCIAL ASSISTANCE	2001/02	2002/03	2003/04	2004/05	2005/06 MTEF	2006/07 MTEF	2007/08 MTEF
Gauteng	81.58	84.96	87.44	87.14	90.23	90.46	91.01
Free State	88.66	90.17	89.98	90.30	91.04	90.75	90.93
Eastern Cape	93.41	94.06	94.25	94.91	95.16	95.08	94.94
KwaZulu-Natal	92.83	93.74	94.42	94.74	93.87	93.86	94.05
Mpumalanga	86.67	86.90	88.66	87.59	91.01	88.07	88.35
North-West	92.19	91.74	92.07	93.33	93.27	93.41	93.68
Northern Cape	87.13	88.24	88.86	88.44	88.23	87.77	87.81
Western Cape	81.90	85.17	86.24	85.76	86.20	86.56	87.00
ALL PROVINCES	**88.05**	**89.37**	**90.24**	**90.28**	**91.13**	**90.75**	**90.97**
PROGRAMME 3: SOCIAL WELFARE							
Gauteng	15.53	12.53	8.72	9.11	6.44	6.35	5.85
Free State	9.11	7.42	7.74	7.44	6.80	6.82	6.49
Eastern Cape	4.89	4.08	4.35	13.38	3.81	3.84	3.87
KwaZulu-Natal	5.22	4.19	4.14	3.81	4.91	4.88	4.78
Mpumalanga	4.50	5.55	4.56	4.88	4.34	7.16	6.74
North-West	6.51	6.38	6.49	4.88	4.92	5.09	5.18
Northern Cape	9.60	8.05	6.87	7.27	7.78	7.60	7.59
Western Cape	13.21	10.48	9.94	9.60	9.90	9.44	8.84
ALL PROVINCES	**8.57**	**7.34**	**6.60**	**7.55**	**6.11**	**6.40**	**6.17**

Source: Provincial Budget Statements 2005/06 and own calculations.

Table 4 shows the real growth rates of the social assistance and social welfare spending between 2001/02 and 2004/05 and over the MTEF. There are large variations among all provinces, making it difficult to conclude anything concrete from the data. A trend in the data is that social assistance growth declines from 2002/03 – 2007/08. Social welfare growth, however, also declines in some provinces during this period. This makes it difficult for provinces to be consistent and effective in the delivery of social welfare services on a year-to-year basis.

TABLE 4: REAL GROWTH SOCIAL ASSISTANCE AND SOCIAL WELFARE BUDGETS

PROGRAMME 2: SOCIAL ASSISTANCE	2002/03	2003/04	2004/05	2005/06 MTEF	2006/07 MTEF	2007/08 MTEF
Gauteng	24.95	30.40	16.01	16.38	7.15	3.67
Free State	31.16	26.68	24.59	15.74	5.36	3.55
Eastern Cape	26.37	24.83	14.09	7.58	6.37	3.21
KwaZulu-Natal	25.2	27.3	26.3	7.7	3.9	2.8
Mpumalanga	20.48	27.30	19.91	15.17	4.22	3.73
North-West	20.0	25.7	21.5	10.0	7.9	4.6
Northern Cape	19.82	20.07	6.49	12.93	4.62	3.47
Western Cape	24.64	15.31	9.73	9.52	1.93	4.43
ALL PROVINCES	24.08	24.70	17.33	11.88	5.18	3.68
PROGRAMME 3: SOCIAL WELFARE						
Gauteng	-3.21	-11.84	21.61	-20.49	5.37	-5.07
Free State	5.08	32.36	19.34	4.91	6.01	-1.64
Eastern Cape	4.56	32.93	248	-69.42	7.32	4.13
KwaZulu-Natal	-0.3	24.8	15.9	40.0	3.3	0.4
Mpumalanga	48.23	2.37	30.01	-1.47	77.78	-2.70
North-West	18.3	27.5	-9.9	11.1	11.4	6.2
Northern Cape	-0.85	1.79	13.28	21.07	2.70	3.39
Western Cape	-4.90	8.02	6.59	12.32	-3.15	-2.69
ALL PROVINCES	8.36	14.74	43.10	-0.25	13.84	0.25

Source: Provincial Budget Statements 2005/06 and own calculations. Note: For the conversion of nominal data into real data (to adjust budgets for inflation), the Gross Domestic Product inflation data provided by Statistics South Africa was used with 2006/07 as a base year.

Figure 1 shows the average annual growth (2001/02 – 2007/08) of both social assistance and social welfare spending and budget allocations. The annual growth rate of the social assistance programmes hovers between 10 and 15% in some provinces, except for the Western Cape and Northern Cape where the annual average growth was below 10%. The social welfare annual growth rate, however, is below 10% in most provinces, except for Mpumalanga and KwaZulu-Natal, which have growth rates of 19% and 11% respectively. Social assistance is growing at a faster rate than that of social welfare across all provinces, except for Mpumalanga.

Avg Annual Growth of Social Assistance & Social Welfare Programmes-2001/02-2007/08

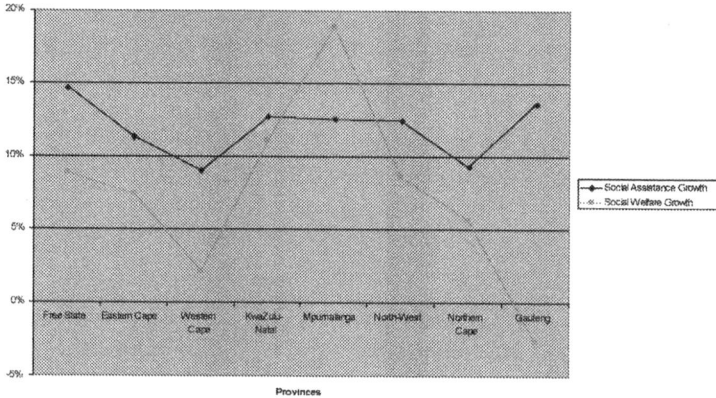

IMPLICATIONS FOR SOCIAL WELFARE SERVICES AND CHILDREN'S RIGHTS

The social assistance programme is the most effective mechanism to alleviate poverty. Even though the main disadvantage of social assistance is that it cannot guarantee that the money will actually be spent on the beneficiaries (Marcus, 2004: 3), it is the only viable mechanism to ensure funds reach the beneficiaries. Poverty-alleviation programmes, however, should address the problem in a comprehensive manner and not simply provide short- or medium-term relief. Poverty alleviation also should deal with the causes and cycle of poverty in which individuals, families and communities are caught. This is the role of social welfare services, but with the crowding out effect of social assistance programmes, which in itself is not sustainable in the long term, social welfare programmes have had to make do with the few resources they have had over the years. This has had serious implications for the social welfare system in meeting children's obligations.

In a recently released report on provincial expenditure trends, the National Treasury expected an annual growth in social welfare services of 20.8% over the 2006/07 – 2008/09 MTEF (National Treasury, 2006: 53). This is encouraging and should be monitored to see if this is in fact a reality in terms of budget allocations. Another encouraging aspect of the report is that social workers' salaries are set to grow at an average annual rate of 21.7% over the MTEF, which is R2.4 billion by 2008/09 (ibid: 54). This should help to retain the existing pool of social workers and attract more over the MTEF.

An aspect of the report that is of concern, however, is the provincial social develop-ment departments' ability to actually spend their full budgets. The preliminary expenditure outcome for the 2005/06 financial year shows that provinces have col-lectively underspent their adjusted budget by 9%, or R416 million. The KwaZulu-Natal's social development department underspent by 17.3%, the most of all the provinces (ibid).

The report also provides an overview of how many children are reached through the child care and protection services sub-programme. First, the average per capita fund-ing for the 2005/06 period for children under this programme was R54, but among provinces this varies greatly, with the Western Cape spending R113 per child, Mpumalanga spending R22 and North-West spending only R18 per child (ibid: 63). Second, the report discloses that there is a shortfall of the current levels of service delivery, with demand for services outstripping what is supplied. At present this programme reaches almost 500 000 children through support services in children's homes and subsidised and non-subsidised crèches (ibid) but, as noted before, more than 11 million children live in poverty and need the necessary services.

Streak and Poggenpoel (2005: 44) identified several challenges in social welfare service delivery:

- Lack of reliable information on social welfare service delivery across provinces;
- Inconsistencies in the planning and implementation of social welfare services across provinces;
- Role-players, inside and outside of social development departments, have different understandings of what social welfare services are and how they should be transformed; and
- Social development departments and their NGO partners have varying capacities across provinces to implement the transformation vision.

All of these challenges have serious consequences for the delivery of social welfare services and for how they meet the obligations for children's rights. Already, in terms of social welfare delivery, the social development departments are not reaching all children in need. With government plans to make social welfare a priority over the MTEF, it is important that it tackles two of its main challenges head on. First, social development departments need to find mechanisms to retain, attract and equip social workers within the government and the NGO sectors and, second, provincial social development departments need to increase their capacity to plan and implement the required services. The, latter, however, will require guidance and support from the national Department of Social Development to implement the new vision of social developmental welfare services.

REFERENCES

Children's Institute, 2006. *Children Count – Abantwana Babalulekile*, Accessed at www.childrencount.ci.org.za

Leatt, A. 2006. *Grants for Children: A Brief Look at the Eligibility and Take-Up of the Child Support Grant and Other Cash Grants*, Children's Institute Working Paper Number 5. Cape Town: Children's Institute, University of Cape Town.

Marcus, R. 2004. *The Role of Cash Transfers in Tackling Childhood Poverty*, CHIP Policy Briefing 2, London: CHIP.

National Department of Social Development, 2006. *Service Delivery Model for Developmental Social Services*, January, 2006.

National Department of Social Development, 2006. *Strategic Plan of the Department of Social Development, 2006/07 – 2009/10*.

National Treasury, 2006. *Provincial Budgets and Expenditure Review: 2002/03 – 2008/09*, www.treasury.gov.za

Rosa, S. & Dutschke, M. 2006. *Child Rights at the Core: A Commentary on the Use of International Law in South African Court Cases on Children's Socio-Economic Rights*, A Project 28 Working Paper, Cape Town: Children's Institute, University of Cape Town.

Streak, J. 2004a. *Government Spending on Children in MTEF 2004-05: Spotlighting Social Development Programmes*, Cape Town: Budget Information Service, IDASA.

Streak, J. & Wehner, J. 2004b. "Children's Socio-Economic Rights in the South African Constitution: Towards a Framework for Monitoring Implementation," in *Monitoring Child Socio-Economic Rights in South Africa*, (eds.), Coetzee, E. & Streak, J, Cape Town: Children's Budget Unit, IDASA.

Streak, J. & Poggenpoel, S. 2005c. *Towards Social Welfare Services for All Vulnerable Children in South Africa: A Review of Policy Development, Budgeting and Service Delivery*, Cape Town: Budget Information Service, IDASA.

Streak, J. 2005d. *Provincial Budgets for Developmental Social Welfare Services Over MTEF 2005/06: A Vulnerable Child Perspective*, Cape Town: Budget Information Service, IDASA.

APPENDIX: SEMINAR PARTICIPANTS
(as at October 2005)

Dr Miriam Altman
Executive Director, Employment & Economic Policy Research, HSRC

Ms Carol Bower
Executive Director, RAPCAN

Dr Rachel Bray
Research Fellow, Centre for Social Science Research, UCT

Ms Shaamela Cassiem
Unit Manager, Children's Budget Unit, IDASA

Ms Erika Coetzee
Freelance writer/materials developer

Mr Neil Coleman
Head of the Parliamentary Office, COSATU

Ms Monet Durieux
Economist, National Treasury

Ms Deborah Ewing
Director, iMediate Development Communications

Prof Johann Fedderke
Professor of Economics, UCT

Mr David Fryer
Lecturer, Economics Department, Rhodes University

Ms Katharine Hall
Senior Researcher, Children's Institute, UCT

Ms Khomotso Kgothadi
Deputy Director, Office on the Rights of the Child, the Presidency

Dr Ellen Kornegay
Chief Director, Programmes, the Presidency

Ms Annie Leatt
Child Poverty Programme Manager, Children's Institute, UCT

Dr Charles Meth
Senior Research Fellow, School of Development Studies, UKZN

Mr Abrahams Mutedi
Executive Manager, Department of Labour

Ms Trine Naeraa-Nicolajsen
Programme Officer, Children's Socio-economic Rights, Save the Children Sweden

Ms Katerina Nicolaou
Director, Labour and UIF, National Treasury

Ms Christina Nomdo
Trainer/Researcher, Children's Budget Unit, IDASA

Mr Elroy E. Paulus
Research Co-Ordinator, COSATU Parliamentary Office

Ms Laura Poswell
Senior Researcher, Development Policy Research Unit, School of Economics, UCT

Ms Mastoera Sadan
Director, Social Sector Policy Coordination and Advisory Services, the Presidency

Ms Judith Streak
Senior Researcher, Children's Budget Unit, IDASA

www.ingramcontent.com/pod-product-compliance
Lightning Source LLC
Chambersburg PA
CBHW080251030426
42334CB00023BA/2774